FROM SELF-CARE TO SELF-MASTERY

An Intimate Journey for Reflection and Action

DR. MONICA STARKE

Copyright © 2024
DR. MONICA STARKE
FROM SELF-CARE TO SELF-MASTERY
An Intimate Journey for Reflection and Action
All rights reserved.

No part of this publication may be reproduced, distributed, or transmitted in any form or by any means, including photocopying, recording, or other electronic or mechanical methods, without the prior written permission of the author, except in the case of brief quotations embodied in critical reviews and certain other non-commercial uses permitted by copyright law.

To request permissions, contact the author at monica@selfmasterysanctuary.com or at www.selfmasterysanctuary.com

DR. MONICA STARKE
Publisher: Monica Starke, Ed.D.

Printed Worldwide
First Printing 2024
First Edition 2024

ISBN IS 979-8-9908502-0-0

10 9 8 7 6 5 4 3 2 1

Editor: Patricia Kyle
Cover Design: Epic Bookcovers

The information provided in this book is based on the author's research and personal experiences. Readers should seek professional advice before making any decisions based on the content of this book. The author and publisher disclaim any liability for any direct or indirect consequences from the use of this book.

The content of this book is for informational purposes only and is not intended to diagnose, treat, cure, or prevent any condition or disease. You understand that this book is not intended as a substitute for consultation with a licensed practitioner. Please consult with your own physician or healthcare specialist regarding the suggestions and recommendations made in this book. The use of this book implies your acceptance of this disclaimer.

DEDICATION

For my five children, my five favorites in order of birth - Tracey, Richard, Lisa, Gena and Andrew, my son-in-law, Joseph, my daughter-in-law, Vonette and my nine amazing grandchildren – Neema, Ariel, Isaac, Isabel, Joseph, Jayden, Elijah, Levi, and Atarah.

For my niece Sandra and my brother, Harold, who never lost faith in my writing.

Finally for my siblings, relatives, friends, colleagues, and clients who are striving to become better self-managers!

"You will always have ups and downs in this life but take time to enjoy all your perfect moments along the way"

— Starke.

TABLE OF CONTENTS

Foreword 1 1
  By My Daughter, Gena Raymond
Foreword 2 3
  By Patricia Kyle
Preface 5
  Your 911 Call to Action!
Introduction 7
Chapter One...13
  Make Wise Choices
Chapter Two 41
  Set Goals You TRUST
Chapter Three 59
  Create Your Sanctuary of Peace
Chapter 4 75
  Use Winning Ways to Talk and Listen
Chapter 5 87
  Maximize Your 24 Hours
Chapter 6 95
  Increase Your Faith
Chapter 7 113
  Become the Ultimate Self-Manager
From Self-Care to Self-Mastery 137
  An Intimate Journey for Reflection and Action

Foreword 1

By My Daughter, Gena Raymond

I've always struggled to find a balance between acceptance and control in my life. To this day, the Serenity Prayer is like an old friend I often call upon. I believe the mystery of a happy life entails knowing what to let go of and when, accepting what we cannot control, and focusing our love, attention, and energy on those aspects of life we can directly influence. It is on this "middle path" where I have found the most joy.

Mummy's book, From Self-Care to Self-Mastery is sure to keep me on this middle path!

Even though the concept is simple, the application is far from easy as we are such complex beings. When my mother first told me about the concept of her new book, the concept of 'amor fati' is what came to mind for me. The book is intended for those who see that 'amor fati' does not mean using surrender as an excuse to give up. It is for those who are ready for the middle path and just need some guidance getting there as we all do sometimes. I believe part of growing from self-care to self-mastery is accepting what we cannot change, but making the most of what we can. You are already on your way to doing that by picking up a book like this.

May it be a part of your North Star to find that good place in life, along with your personal love, knowledge, and intuition to guide you.

With love,

Gena

Foreword 2

By Patricia Kyle

I am still in awe of this amazing piece of literature. The book is one of the best nonfiction books I have read in a long time as an editor. The author is endowed with a strong, creative, and expressive writing style. This book contains salient self-help knowledge that will transform an average individual into a super, high performer.

As a result, it puts the author first in the exalted league of Notable T&T Nonfiction Writers. Monica's ability to capture the depth of her challenging moments and how her endearing spirit, perseverance, and positive choices conquered her challenges left me encouraged and enlightened. Each chapter carefully and concisely made me better and deeply appreciate the process and importance of self-mastery while allowing for a great level of introspection and enlightenment.

I am encouraged by Monica's growth and am in awe of her achievements. Readers will get a firsthand account of the seven strategies guaranteed to transform an average man into a high performer. Also, readers will learn about the compounding impact of little positive choices and how they strongly improve our lives.

Readers will appreciate the importance of setting achievable goals, the benefits of maximizing time, and the impact of self-care and personal time for peaceful introspection. Monica shared the transforming ability of faith in what we do and the life-giving force of human connection. This memoir has captured many occurrences that limit personal development and progress and provided inspiring messages.

Patricia

Preface

Your 911 Call to Action!

I have fallen so many times. But I have always managed to pick myself up.

My faith in God, solid support from a few key people, and my unwavering self-confidence helped me survive and thrive.

In today's challenging, complex, and uncertain environment, you, too, MUST learn how to pick yourself up when you fall.

As I share my perception of these two valuable concepts, I invite you to embark on this journey that will take you from self-care to self-mastery. My seven chapters will make you stronger, bolder, more effective, and more successful! They will enable you to survive, thrive, and find joy amidst the chaos.

Many of us give freely to our children, partners, parents, relatives, friends, neighbors, and even strangers. Yet, we feel reluctant when it's time to spend money on ourselves or to give ourselves the precious gifts of time and self-care. Guilt keeps us back almost every time!

I want to help you realize that taking care of YOU physically, emotionally, mentally, and spiritually is the greatest gift you will ever give to others. Only when your cup is full and overflowing can you be truly present.

Let me help convince, guide, and motivate you with seven transformative steps that enabled me to stay strong despite countless challenges. I urge you to find your 'amor fati' (your formula for a great living) as you adopt the skills and techniques I share—so you, too, will become your best self and see yourself as worthy of everything good.

With love and respect,

Monica

INTRODUCTION

You have probably managed to handle your basic needs despite all the other responsibilities that confront you daily. You work, take care of children and other family members, perform other necessary duties, but barely manage to care for yourself. Hopefully, you will try to eat right, exercise, and secure medical and dental checkups. But would you honestly say that you have achieved those personal and professional goals that you have been thinking or dreaming about?

- Are you personally fulfilled and satisfied with your life?
- Do you wish for more joy?
- Are there some things about your life you want to change? Do you want to become your best self?

If the answer is a resounding 'yes,' I invite you to embark on this journey with me, as we move from self-care to self-mastery. *This will enable you to see yourself as worthy of all possible blessings and the great gifts your life can offer.*

Get excited because you are going to experience self and spiritual development that will encourage and motivate you to become a lifelong learner and an ultimate self-manager. As you navigate our complex and demanding environment, you will become your best self and influence and transform those around you with your unique and amazing self-discovery, renewal, and transformation—through the attainment of self-mastery.

~ ~ ~

I was forced to develop more effective coping skills as I dealt with my various roles and responsibilities as a single parent, daycare owner/director, flight attendant, teacher, school principal, professor, psychotherapist, consultant, mother, grandmother, aunt, friend, and more. I learned to go from being a dependent person to an independent woman and professional. I finally captured and understood the immense value of an interdependent existence that taught me the value of support from others for the achievement of a successful transformation.

Therefore, I am very grateful to all those who supported my journey from self-care to self-mastery. "My cup runneth over" with gratitude! (Psalm 23:5-6).

"Gratitude is not just good medicine, though, a nice sentiment, a warm fuzzy feeling, or a strategy or tactic for being happier or healthier. It is also the truest approach to life. We did not create or fashion ourselves, and we did not get to where we are in life by ourselves. So, living in gratitude is living in truth. It is the most accurate and honest approach to life,"

— Dr. Robert A. Emmons

That support system included my adult children, family members, colleagues, mentors, and especially my doctoral students from Nova Southeastern University (NSU), whom I enjoyed serving for twenty years. From these adult learners, I learned more about the importance of self-mastery during the formal and informal surveys that consistently pointed out that self-mastery was the essential quality necessary for genuine personal and professional development and for their future leadership roles.

Many verbal answers and twenty-page papers provided research to sustain their ardent belief in self-mastery. Initially, I thought they would have cited knowledge of technology as the greatest need for future leaders, but I was happy that this expectation was incorrect. When we teach, indeed, we also learn so much! Malcolm Knowles, lovingly known as the father of andragogy (adult learning), will undoubtedly agree with this statement.

~ ~ ~

My definition of self-mastery:

"How to dig deep and become acutely aware of YOUR unique, God-given gifts, talent, and skills, to fully recognize the power you have to utilize the strengths that are still hidden in your secret space, your inner spirit," is my description of self-mastery.

Right now is the perfect time to let YOUR light shine!

"Let your light so shine before men, that they may see your good works, and glorify your Father which is in heaven"

— *(Matthew 5:16).*

It's time to discover a NEW YOU. It's time to become your best SELF and the ultimate SELF-MANAGER by adopting my seven proven self-mastery strategies.

"A Journey of a thousand miles begins with a single step"

— Lao Tzu

7 Steps to Self Mastery

1. Make Wise Choices
2. Set Goals You Can Trust
3. Create Your Sanctuary of Peace
4. Use Winning Ways to Talk and Listen
5. Maximise Your 24 Hours
6. Increase Your Faith
7. Become the Ultimate Self-Manager

Chapter One

Make Wise Choices

Understand the Power of a Choice

How are you doing right now? Are you coping well or struggling through each day feeling anxious and fearful? Maybe you wake up and wonder how to get through the day because you feel unmotivated and a little lost. Maybe you feel great most days and experience those negative thoughts and feelings only on certain days.

At whatever point in your life this book reaches you, I hope all I share will enable you to gain greater strength, increased wisdom, and inner peace that will last for your lifetime. These powerful tools will enable you to overcome each challenge that confronts you with the necessary grace to live fully and intentionally.

"Life is a matter of choices, and every choice you make makes you,"

— John C. Maxwell

Recognize this Power to Choose Comes from God

As adults, we consistently face choices. Often, choosing will involve unavoidable pain and distress that will require us to grow—once we decide to confront and solve the problems that will come into our lives. We are unable to escape from this reality.

Still, I would not be willing to give up my ability to choose. Remember that one of our greatest God-given gifts is our ability and freedom to make our own choices! Therefore, the choice to change and seize opportunities to learn, grow, and make positive changes is yours. Make them with God's help and guidance.

Once you choose to change, the next step would be to make a commitment. Making those choices to grow and change requires fierce commitment, which will be the secret to your success.

The freedom to choose is a powerful gift we should appreciate and value. This does not, however, diminish the fact that many decisions will be painful and even cause some suffering. Remember that adversity can initiate tremendous growth. Let us acknowledge and celebrate that we have the power to find solutions with God's help because if we don't, we will be lost. Hold on to that power as you make your choices to grow and make decisions to become better.

Use Your Energy and Wisdom to Focus on Possible Solutions!

I was confronted with making very tough decisions when I was twenty years old. I was still innocent and unwise and became pregnant with my first child. I was then teaching in a Catholic school, and it was understood that if you got pregnant, you got married as long as the father was willing. Although my excellent doctor offered me an abortion, I chose to have my child without hesitation, fully aware that this was the more difficult option. The support of my family helped when my young husband departed for Holland to seek a better life, and I became a single mother for many years.

There was pain but no regrets—only tremendous growth!

Later, I was faced with another very painful choice. When my daughter was almost four, I became a flight attendant with British West Indian Airways (BWIA). I loved being a flight attendant, but after seven years of leaving my daughter in the care of her loving grandmother, the tantrums that ensued each time I had to leave told me that she had endured enough of my departures. It took courage, and I suffered throughout the decision to quit my wonderful job. But I did. No regrets, only wonderful growth!

I hope you, too, will cultivate the courage to endure the decision-making process and the strength to follow this with action! Making wise decisions and choices will involve patience and pain. However, I tell my children that pain and suffering indicate we are making wise choices—and not making willy-nilly decisions.

Poor Choices Always Appear to be Much Easier.

Today, if you have made poor choices that cause you to live in misery, dare to make a change. Muster the courage to begin to make those difficult choices despite the pain. Many amazing opportunities and tremendous personal and spiritual growth will emerge.

"One can choose to go back towards safety forward towards growth. Growth must be chosen again and again; fear must be overcome again and again."

— *Abraham Maslow*

Begin with Self-Care

The greatest gift we can give others is taking care of our health so we can live as long and as well as we can. This means eating well, exercising, keeping up with regular doctors' visits, getting enough sleep and rest, and making sure that we are thriving physically, socially, psychologically, professionally, emotionally, and financially.

FROM SELF-CARE TO SELF-MASTERY

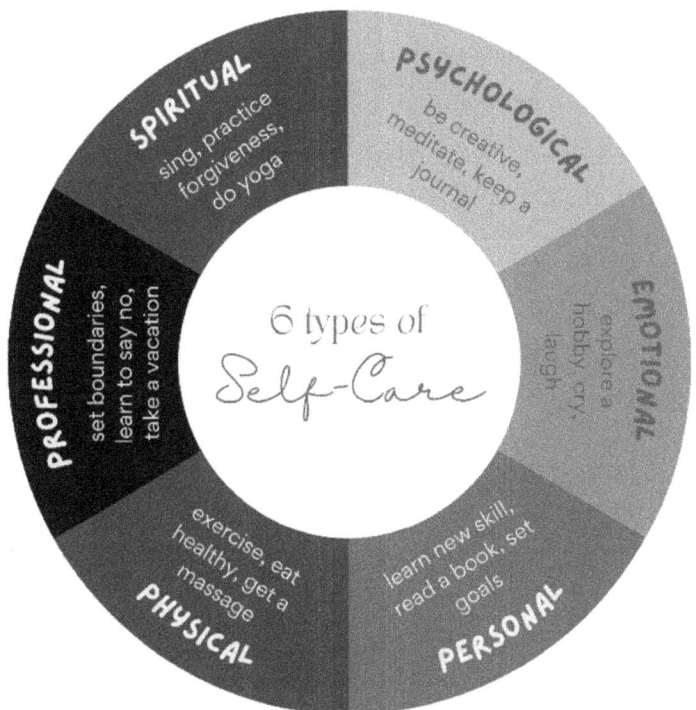

Our loved ones want us to live fully by enjoying good health and experiencing many moments of joy. We should take care of our bodies and our minds, and we should do so without guilt. Good self-care is an unselfish practice. Even the Bible, the best-selling book in the world, urges us to "love thy neighbor as thyself." We should all put in the necessary effort to self-care. Make wise choices because the quality of self-care in our younger years can determine how we age.

But can we really achieve all the above without being excellent self-managers?

Taking care of ourselves, as described above, is a tall order and one that we can pursue more effectively with growth and self-improvement. To grow and develop into our best selves, there needs to be a particular focus on achieving self-mastery that involves serious and continuous self-development.

This unique quality of self-development also involves spiritual development. In fact, they go hand in hand because when the body and the mind are developed, it's a slam dunk, and I call this the attainment of self-mastery.

Excel with Self-Mastery

When you become the ultimate self-manager, you can become your best self, a person with that inner strength of body and spirit who can stay strong and stand tall in the face of adversity.

This kind of growth must surely come because life is filled with ups and downs, pain and joy, perfect and imperfect moments, so the ability to be resilient in the face of adversity is necessary. Ultimate self-managers will fall from time to time but will always have the resolve to pick themselves up without turning to drugs, alcohol, or violence.

Good self-care is the right beginning, but self-mastery provides a natural high and a journey that permits us to experience another level, a deeper level of joy, wisdom, and countless perfect moments.

~ ~ ~

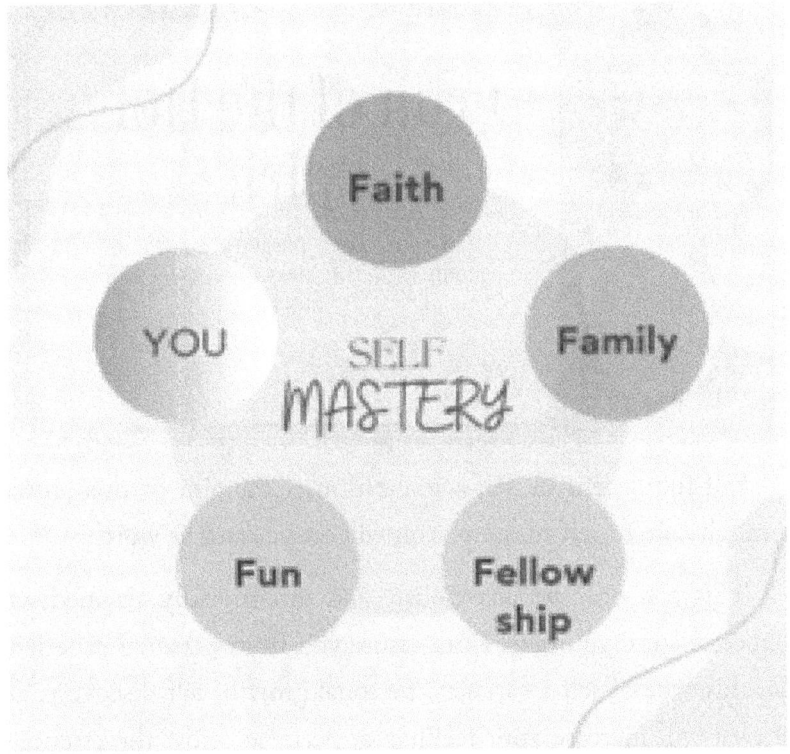

Remember that this journey is continuous; we should never stop learning and growing. This journey is beautiful and fulfilling once we have the desire and humility to be always open to growth and positive change.

We can all strive to live according to the fruit of the Holy Spirit as provided in the Bible—and below. The seven steps I provide in this little book help.

Self-fulfillment or self-actualization is the aim of this journey from self-care to self-mastery. You will see yourself as worthy!

This can only be consciously and intentionally attained with deliberate steps you take! I can assure you from personal experience that this type of self-awareness, personal growth, self-discovery, and renewal will increase your feelings of peace and joy, the essence of human existence.

> *"This is the single most powerful investment we can ever make in life — investment in ourselves, in the only instrument we have with which to deal with life and to contribute..."*
>
> *— Scott Peck*

Change Requires Risk

I have paid high prices for my growth and development and taken risks to the point where some friends and family members often called me 'crazy.' Call it self-love, but I love my disposition despite the tears and the pain growth and change have caused me.

After seven years as a flight attendant, I separated from my second husband and had to find a way to support myself and my children quickly. Although I had no experience setting up or managing a daycare center, I realized that if I faced the dilemma of working and taking care of kids, other parents probably had the same problem.

I was dead right and decided to act.

I quit flying and opened a daycare center that was very successful. However, after two years, I realized that I could help the kids and parents a great deal more if I were the psychotherapist I always dreamed about being. There were so many problems!

A choice began to develop in my brain after a fateful meeting with the director of international recruitment at the University of Miami (UM). I had secured an opportunity to be part of a morning show called 'Community Dateline' on Trinidad and Tobago's (T&T) national television station and was assigned to interview Ms. Debra Triole Perry, who was in T&T to recruit prospective students for UM. After the interview, she gave me her card and casually said, "If you are ever in Miami, call me."

That night, I could not sleep as I could visualize the possibility of fulfilling my long-term goal, but I was concerned about losing my business. As an absent business owner, the risk was significant.

After carefully weighing the pros and cons, I decided to take it anyway because the rewards of this choice could dramatically change my life for the better.

Although I was keenly aware of the risks, I decided to leave my excellent manager in charge of my business. My mother agreed to help me obtain a coveted green card so I could become a resident of the United States.

By this time, I had secured a divorce from my second husband, who supported my leaving the country to study. I confronted the opportunity and the risk, sold my car and a few other possessions, went to Florida to meet with Debra, and registered to start my undergraduate degree at age thirty-two.

I was terrified but very excited.

As an ex-flight attendant, I was known by the BWIA crew members on the flight from T & T to Miami. I was armed with my now four young children and my elderly mother, who had sponsored my green card and had also kindly agreed to stay with me for a while as I settled in Florida. The flight to Miami had to stop in Puerto Rico, and the US rule was that you cleared immigration at that first US port. The process for the six of us naturally took a while, and the flight was delayed because of us. I should have been embarrassed, but I don't recall feeling so. What I do remember as we walked to our seats, somewhat oblivious of the stares from other passengers, is the remark from my former colleague, the chief flight attendant, who said to me, "Girl, I don't know whether I should admire you or whether to think you are crazy." I couldn't respond then, nor did I care to do so. I wasn't surprised that she thought I was "crazy."

I was in the middle of this enormous life change.

If this was crazy, it was worth my anticipation and excitement about fulfilling my dream of becoming a psychotherapist since I was seventeen and childless. That colleague continued to fly until she was in her sixties and then retired quietly in Trinidad. I went on to get my doctorate and become a psychotherapist and professor despite my crazy aspirations. I would choose crazy again and again!

> *"Don't worry if people think you're crazy. You are crazy. You have that kind of intoxicating insanity that lets other people dream outside of the lines and become who they're destined to be."*

— Jennifer Elisabeth, <u>Born Ready: Unleash Your Inner Dream Girl</u>

Freedom to choose is a precious gift, and if you dare to choose the complex paths that involve growth and change, I can tell you it is worth every ounce of pain and self-sacrifice—if you decide to fulfill your deepest wishes. You do not have to depend on others to make wise choices about your life.

Tears will be shed, but the joy accompanying the pain can be utterly fulfilling, and those choices will change your life—for the better!

Dare to be exactly you. See yourself as worthy. Remember that sometimes you must leap into the unfamiliar to discover your unique self and achieve spiritual development. This can make you a total man or woman and will capture your essence as a capable, confident, and independent individual.

Sometimes, we derive the greatest joy and satisfaction when we do not conform to others' expectations. If you fear pain, you will consciously or unconsciously avoid growth and positive change, but where is the fun in that?

The essence of life is the ability to detect when we are experiencing our perfect moments. We must be willing to suffer through tough times. When we overcome these, the joy flows, and this injection of drug-free exuberance induces the greatest highs of our human existence.

When we learn to allow ourselves to be open to experience pain and joy freely, we live fully and grow emotionally and spiritually. Then, we are strong enough to face anything without fear—even death. We now see ourselves as worthy.

"Joy awakens all our senses, energizing mind, and body. Both gratitude and joy reflect a fully alive, alert, and awake state of attunement between the self and the world, which is necessary for sustainable well-being,"

— *Dr. Robert A. Emmons*

Like so many people, my children and grandchildren don't like any conversations that may include the topic of dying. I often remind them, "Dying is part of living." This is my gentle reminder as I genuinely would like them to be aware of the reality of death. Then, their perception of death may not be an unfamiliar phenomenon but one that is always present, natural, unavoidable, inescapable, and a vital part of living fully.

I hope this awareness that we do not have forever will encourage and motivate them—and you—to overcome the grip of fear and become excited and accommodating about growth and change. Along the way, make every effort to satisfy the deep desires of your heart, but always try to act in ways that honor our heavenly Father. This will enable you to see yourself as worthy.

Change Requires Courage

My life has been filled with pain, but I have lived fully and have enjoyed so many perfect moments!

There were many times when I could have made better decisions, but I am grateful that instead of focusing on what I should have done, I learned from each mistake and tried to improve every time. I do have one regret—that my children have different last names because I ended up being officially married three times. I do not regret the marriages, but I feel so strongly about family that I wish we could have been the Starkes, the Cotterills, or the Rabathalys. Despite this regret and the hardships along the way, I have managed to build a strong and diverse family unit. Above all, I see myself as worthy of every perfect moment I can muster.

I would choose my painful choices again and again to live as fully as I have.

Interestingly, my maiden name was Hendrie, but I took and kept my first husband's last name, Starke—simply because I liked it and selfishly because I liked the sound of Monica Starke and planned to use it when I became a writer, which was one of my long-term goals. Fortunately, my second and third husbands never objected. I guess they knew that I would keep it anyway.

According to my mother, I have been making my own decisions since the age of four and have never stopped. I have not always made the best decisions, but I figured that if I made them, I was prepared to live with the consequences—good or bad.

My mother shared that originally, my first name was Martha, and at four, I informed her and my other six siblings that, moving forward, they were to call me Monica.

I insisted, and I clearly remember that when I had to attend school formally at eight after being homeschooled, my mom and I went to an attorney's office to have my name formally changed. Looking back, I believe that my fiercely independent way of thinking and my persistence in making my own decisions were the primary reasons for difficulties in my marriages.

Honestly, I have no regrets except for the one I shared earlier, although my independence and freedom have not been without self-sacrifice.

I am extremely thankful that my children still find it in their hearts to love and respect me for who I am. They realize that I have always put them first, and I am so grateful that my son calls me "the best mommy in the world" consistently, while one of my daughters told me today that it was very easy to love me. I am thankful I have always chosen to look on the bright side of situations. This has saved me on many occasions, and a positive outlook will save you, too.

In one of my favorite books, "The Road Less Traveled," psychiatrist Dr. Scott Peck puts it this way: "Move out or grow in any dimension, and pain, as well as joy, will be your reward. A full life will be full of pain. But the only alternative is not to live fully or not to live at all."

Let me share a significant and challenging change I recently made to elicit the self-discipline and courage I needed to edit and publish the few books I have been writing.

Like so many, I love a good movie or a good series. These just take you away from the present, and we could all use this escape during these turbulent times—but making a sensible choice is not always easy. This may have been a fun choice and may sound like a simple challenge, but I will confess that drastically decreasing my time spent with news and Netflix was extremely difficult.

Don't be mistaken. I have not given up news and Netflix altogether, but the decrease needed to be significant. I am so thankful I had the will to take back so much of my time to spend on what I hope to be my legacy—sharing my lessons learned to help you live your best life.

Change Can Take Time

Change can be very painful and messy, but if we endure, it can happen, and situations can improve, even if this happens slowly, over months and years. Relationships can be very challenging—we see this all the time. However, we should never give up because relationships can improve if we keep making those sincere and serious efforts.

As I shared earlier, I had my beautiful daughter, my first child, when I was twenty. When she was ten years old, she threw tantrums whenever I left to go on a flight. Hence, I decided to quit, got married again, and had two more children. Although her new dad and I made every effort to include her in the family, she never felt truly accepted.

This lack of a stable and healthy relationship with my eldest daughter has been very difficult and challenging. Although it seemed like she would never feel as loved as my other children, I have spent years re-examining my parenting practices and improving my parenting efforts to make her feel as loved and appreciated as she was and still is.

For the last year, I have finally stopped feeling guilty and making strenuous and expensive efforts to show her how much she is valued. This change was painful and came after many years, but it brought a sense of enormous emotional relief when I finally made the conscious decision to let go of my guilt.

I will continue loving her like I love my other children—gracefully and effortlessly. Now, she must also make changes and try to find the peace and love that I offer, and I do feel that she is finally doing so. Our relationship has improved over the years, and I celebrate every small victory and will continue to hope for more. We are doing so much better! I never gave up.

Change requires perseverance

Some changes are bigger and more complex than others, and complete transformation and success may never happen. Sometimes, we may have to settle and be grateful for the small successes. Change requires perseverance.

You will be glad when you persist because the alternative is no way to live!

I fully understand the misery that comes along with complex decision-making. I want to help you rebuild and transform those negative, self-defeating woes to regain and reclaim your emotional and spiritual strength by sharing the strategies that have worked so well for me. These have left me standing tall despite many pitfalls I encountered throughout my life.

All of us have joyful days. We can face those days with strength and hope.

But some days, we just want to stay in our beds. We want to be left alone. We want the world to go away. This is acceptable for a few hours, a day, maybe even a few days—but not longer. You may need to seek professional help if those feelings persist, but I want you to reach the point when you will be able to cope with whatever life throws at you.

You might get knocked down, but you will be able to use the seven steps I share to regain your personal power and stand tall in the face of any life challenge. You will be able to face most days with purpose, passion, a clearer vision, and an attitude of gratitude.

On that day when you cannot do so, it is probably a sign that you need to take some time out.

When you do, the next day is usually much brighter because you have not surrendered your power to make new choices. You are now willing to confront any sense of helplessness and acquire the ability to cope. You have accepted that to live fully and responsibly means to accept that we will always need to make wise choices for growth and joyful change. Persist, keep on going, be determined, don't give up!

Set Aside Time for Reflection and Self-Examination

Self-examination is essential, but it certainly isn't always an easy process. In fact, sometimes it can be downright painful, especially if we are going to be very honest. If you are serious about achieving self-mastery, I urge you to develop a willingness to be open to the practice of regular self-examination. I was so pleased to learn that Dr. Scott Peck agrees with me. In his book, "The Road Less Traveled," he states that we must have "the willingness and the capacity to suffer continual self-examination."

Let me provide some guidelines for this process.

Set aside a few minutes, a few hours, or days at a place and time that will work for you. Choose whatever will be best for your current situation as you start the process of self-examination. Feel free to use my checklist provided at the end of this chapter.

Take some time out for yourself! Make it happen. Perhaps you are not in a situation to set aside this time immediately—but with some planning and maybe even a few sacrifices, you can invest an hour or two to preserve the well-being of a very important person—you. Before you can move forward, it is necessary to carefully identify those areas of your life that bring you joy and those that need to improve or change. Agree?

Using my guide provided at the end of this chapter, I urge you to invest enough time in self-examination because you know what? You are the most important person in someone's life or maybe the most crucial person in the lives of many people—at home, at work, in your place of worship, and in the community. Therefore, you need to do this for them and you. People who genuinely love you, want you to do well, and take good care of yourself.

You also need to do it because you want to make a change, or maybe a few changes. Unless you are completely satisfied with every aspect of your life, summon the courage to make a few alterations, starting today.

This is not a rehearsal. This is your life, and you have the power to modify your current habits so you can begin to live to your fullest potential and handle today's life challenges more intentionally. Sometimes, all we need is someone—hopefully, me—to tell you that you should and can live your best life. I hope that you will!

Make Self-Examination Simple

Isn't it worth it to take some much-needed time to do some serious and honest self-examination? Yes, or no? You don't have to go to a fancy retreat place with a spa to do so; however, go if you can! You can take some time off and spend it right at home. When last did you do this? You can visit a relative who would make you feel good and allow you some time alone. You can stay at an inexpensive hotel or some distance away. Or, you know what? You can do what I love to do and stay right in your own home, in your room, and in your bed while taking a complete day—just for you. The message here is to take the time to look at yourself and to set a few goals (Chapter 3 will help) to get you started on this journey. After all, don't we always have to do some planning when we take a trip?

I believe that during my life challenges (and there have been many!), taking the time to replenish my body, mind, and spirit has saved me repeatedly.

I have taken minutes to just look at the sky or enjoy the smell of the just-cut grass. I have just stayed in the car listening to my favorite song, which always seems to come on when I arrive at some destination. I have taken the time to watch a complete movie in which I could lose myself or one that would make me laugh out loud (not watching it from the middle or in increments as I do on many occasions). I have also taken half-days or full days (don't get into trouble with your supervisor), stayed in my pajamas (my favorite), slept, reflected, read, watched movies, or walked. Taking time to do absolutely nothing is still one of my favorite things to keep my sanity.

I call these times my "perfect moments."

If you do not spend time with yourself, try it, starting today. I want you to start having as many wonderful moments as you can. I cannot promise that your life will be perfect, but I can promise that you can have many "perfect moments."

Suppose you try, but you can't get away. What can you do?

Get away right there where you are; do the self-exam in increments. Do it while you are at the playground with your little ones; do it while you wait at the doctor's office; do it while you walk with the baby's stroller; do it in the shower; do it just before you go to bed or even while you are in bed—but please do it.

Begin With Small, Deliberate Changes

Maybe it will take some courage to make a start but remember that when we step out of our comfort level, actual change takes place.

Taking this first step by allowing yourself to become open to growth and positive change is always the most challenging part of the journey, but amazing things happen once we do so. Begin to do things you have not done before; it can be something small to start with—like just sitting and having that cup of coffee or tea. A glass of lemon water or lemonade, even a martini or a glass of wine (my favorites), can really help us relax and reflect. Whatever you have, insist on a pretty glass. This makes everything taste better.

Use Time Wisely

Take a book instead of just waiting in misery when you are at the doctor's office. Yes, join the library or get your favorite app and begin to read or listen to books you have thought of reading, books you have always wanted to read but never did. Reading means growth for you and those around you, and you will become a role model for growth and change. Join a reading group, and if you don't know of one, start one with a group of friends and/or family. I can guarantee that this will change your life; you will begin to have a deeply satisfying life. When you accomplish this, everyone benefits!

Prioritize! Prioritize!

Space out your tasks or chores in order of need. Don't aim to do everything at once. Reschedule as often as you need, depending on the importance. This is **your** priority list. No one is there to judge you. Get the items done in the most creative and efficient ways. 'Prioritize' sounds cliche, but this process works. Prioritize! Enjoy the act of deleting, ticking, or drawing a line through when a task, action, or goal is completed.

If I am not having a high-energy day, I often review my list and ask myself, "OK, let's see what has to be done today?" On days when my energy is high, I try to do twice or three times as much. I am not acting according to my feelings. I am utilizing my energy effectively!

I also reward myself when I extend my energy to complete a task. That good feeling of erasing the task is great, but it's so important to celebrate. I celebrate everything, not always in significant ways with shopping or champagne but sometimes with a glass of wine and/or a movie, or anything else that makes you feel rewarded. Learn to tap your own shoulder!

Exercise Consistently

Start exercising regularly, as you have always wanted to do. I know this takes effort, but it is so worth it! Although this can be fun, you don't have to join a gym. You can start as I did—by walking at least twenty minutes daily at least three times a week. Exercise really makes me feel great and enhances my sense of well-being. I can attest to that… it is not just talk. Be bold and deliberate in your small actions; soon, you will be able to be brave and intentional in every effort as needed.

So, make a start, and whether it's in the shower, while you drive, just before you fall asleep, when you walk, or when you first awake—ask yourself whether you are fully living the life you are privileged to have. Many people don't live to the stage you are at right now.

Don't take your life or your health for granted. About twenty years ago, I thought that I would never be able to touch my toes again. I was in so much pain for months, and it was painful and challenging to climb into bed, get into my car, and even sit or shower. I grieved because I could not put on stockings and thought I would never wear high heels again. I had been to a few doctors, took x-rays and other tests, and the pain persisted; no diagnosis could be made.

Once again, armed with faith in God and myself, I decided to go on a diet of very healthy food and increased exercise. This meant consistent walking and going to a gym for strength training. On days when the pain was not too debilitating, I started to walk more. I increased my intake of fruit and vegetables, and of course, I prayed more and discovered beautiful psalms that I hadn't known before. Changes can be exhilarating.

After one month, I felt strong enough to wear heels, and one week after that, I could wear pantyhose for the first time in a year while facilitating a retreat for an excellent team in West Palm Beach, Florida. My participants had no idea how much I meant it when I urged them to guard their health vigilantly.

Strive for Fulfillment

There is nothing like being at a place in your life when you feel "completely" fulfilled, emotionally and spiritually, at least on most days. You probably already know what it's like to feel empty, lonely, and worn out—somewhat of an empty vessel, perhaps? Although we may never attain "complete" fulfillment, we are human, after all. However, let's try to get as close as possible. Let's find out what it will take to "complete" **you.**

So, now is the time for you to discover the deep satisfaction of knowing that whatever challenge comes your way, you will feel empowered to face it and handle it calmly and directly. Now is the time to become the ultimate self-manager! It is time to discover the "amor fati" for your unique life and affirm that your life is worth living with purpose and passion.

You deserve it if you can take a half-day or a full day for self-examination. Remember that the journey you are about to make will change not only your life but the lives of all those around you—at home, in the office, and in your community—through a ripple effect.

Sometimes, just by 'being,' we influence others.

I worked as a training consultant in an international law firm for five years, and I recall one of the legal assistants saying she missed me because I was absent from work the day before we had that conversation. Although this was about twenty years ago, she said something inspirational; I still remember her saying, "I just feel better when I know you are present on the eighteenth floor." Be that person whose presence becomes a blessing to others.

Don't Give Up

Remember that self-examination is a process that can be painful because you have allowed your life's stressful events to control you instead of the opposite—but you are not alone. It happens to all of us at some time. The important thing is to get back on track before it's too late. Decide to grow and change, and I'll be with you every step of the way as you read each chapter.

Maybe this journey is painful because you have more significant challenges than you care to admit. Perhaps you have severed your relationships with loved ones or have ruined your relationships because of alcohol abuse, neglect, infidelity, or violence. Whatever it is, I assure you that I have seen firsthand that people can make changes that even I never thought possible—for one reason—they wanted to.

Just be open to growth and change with all your heart. That is the first step!

The second step is to be keenly aware of the changes you want to make. Hence, my next chapter is on setting your goals! I am very excited to share. But first....

Are you ready for this critical process of self-examination?

Just place a ✓ or an X in the appropriate circle to indicate your choice. Use this as a guide. Have fun with it.

- o   Am I satisfied with my current level of self-care?
- o   Am I satisfied with my current attitude towards each of my family members?
- o   Am I satisfied with my current attitude towards each person in my inner circle?
- o   Am I currently motivated enough to make the changes I desire?
- o   Have I spent sufficient time identifying the changes I want/need to make?
- o   Have I done a good self-examination?
- o   Am I prepared to become a lifelong learner to understand my behaviors and motivations better?

- o Will I commit to reserving the time for this critical process?
- o Do I have a sound support system?
- o Have I clarified the transformation I want and need?

"The beautiful thing about learning is that nobody can take it away from you."

— *B.B. King*

Here are seven great reminders about why we should all strive to be life-long learners!

1. "The more that you read, the more things you will know. The more that you learn, the more places you'll go."

    — Dr. Seuss

2. "In learning you will teach, and in teaching you will learn."

    — Phil Collins

3. "Learning never exhausts the mind."

    — Leonardo da Vinci

4. "Wisdom…. comes not from age, but from education and learning."

    — Anton Chekhov

5. "I am always doing that which I cannot do, in order that I may learn how to do it."

    — Pablo Picasso

6. "Learn as if you were not reaching your goal and as though you were scared of missing it."

    — Confucius

7. "Intellectual growth should commence at birth and cease only at death."

    — Albert Einstein

Chapter Two

Set Goals You Trust

Have you done your self-exam and come up with a few changes you would like to make? A gentle reminder to write them down! Come up with at least two or three. You probably feel weary from being told you need to have life goals. Try not to be because goal setting works, primarily when you practice the self-discipline required for the process to be successful. Remember to set short-term and long-term goals when you are ready.

Whether the changes you hope to make are minor or profound, your journey will now start with that decisive first step you take. Now is the time to be bold and confident while you step into spaces where you have not dared to go before. You will now try new ways to accomplish the dreams you have hidden in your heart.

I once had a secret dream about being a psychotherapist. When I dared to share this with my family after graduating from high school at age seventeen, they asked, "Who is going to pay for that?" A single mother raised me with seven other children on the island of Trinidad, and life was very tough for her, so I understood. I was disappointed but not angry. I went to the American embassy to inquire about possible scholarships in the United States but soon realized that this was far-fetched, and help was not available then. I want to remind you that I never gave up and held that dream in my heart for almost fifteen years! Long-term goals do get fulfilled.

In January of 1983, at thirty-two years old, I started classes at the University of Miami. I was on my way to fulfilling my long-term goal of being a psychotherapist. My message here is that it's good to have long-term goals because they can become a reality. If you arm yourself with faith in God and hold on to your courage and self-confidence, you can fulfill your goals and dreams despite obstacles and naysayers. Researchers have also found that when people practice gratitude, they become more successful.

"Gratitude is one of the sweet shortcuts to finding peace of mind and happiness inside,"

— *Barry Neil Kaufman*

Review and Redesign Your Goals as Often as Necessary

If you want to make a few changes, consider what areas you need and want to be different. Review and redesign your life goals as necessary and as many times as you choose. Develop your personal path and create and set clear goals that will guide you on your unique journey. Self-discipline is an essential tool as we move forward, and

Dr. Scott Peck reminds us that "The unceasing practice of discipline leads to mastery."

After this self-examination and goal-setting process, you should feel proud of this accomplishment. I applaud you for identifying and clarifying the positive changes you will address.

We are all born with our aspirations and ambitions. We seem to know what we want to achieve but don't always make the choices that support our wishes. Sometimes, we allow life and people to control us and our actions instead of vice versa. Granted, there are some things that we cannot control, but surely, we always want to maintain some measure of freedom over our own lives, and we also want to make our life choices with the full awareness that for each choice we make, we alone will have to live with the consequences.

Therefore, making wise choices that complement our aspirations and ambitions is best. Sometimes we benefit when our goals are not fulfilled precisely when or how we want. This delayed gratification can help us grow. I would not erase the years spent teaching, flying, running a business, or having my children before attaining my long-term goal. The life experiences and the hardships and challenges I endured only served to help me become a more effective psychotherapist and a better person, one with increased faith in God and greater self-confidence. If you are experiencing a delay, remember that this can work in your favor, as I discuss at the end of this chapter.

To make wise choices, we must set goals. This goal-setting process will clarify paths for us to achieve and succeed—if we become experts at setting short-term and long-term goals. Strive to maintain what has become my favorite F word: Flexibility during the goal-setting process.

For instance, one of my short-term goals is to exercise every day because, as my dear niece, a fitness and nutrition expert whose business name is CRIX, told me, "Well, we eat every day, so we need to exercise every day." This might be my desire and my goal, but between us, on the odd day that I am just not up to it, I will excuse myself. Having said this, I will also confess that if on those days I push myself and, with some extra prayers and effort, I manage to accomplish even a portion of the workout or walk or swim as I usually do, I always feel so great and so thankful that I made the extra effort. On the day you are just unable, forgive yourself and strive to do better and be better. That's all we can do! The practice of self-discipline helps.

Understand the Power of Perception

I am confident that you realize we live in a very complex world where so much is constantly changing. How you perceive the world will determine the quality of life you will have. Don't let what is going on in the world at large constantly perplex you since it could prevent you from living your best life. It is advisable to be aware of what is happening, so peek at your environment. Read, listen to the news, and have those water-cooler conversations, but don't stay in that external world for too long. That can be daunting. In his book, 'Everyday in His Presence,' Dr. Charles Stanley reminds us that help is available from a higher power:

"Do you trust God to be your security today? Do you keep your eyes on Him instead of the world situation—the country's mounting debt, the increasing political and spiritual division among people, or the constant threat of terrorist attack? If you take your eyes off God and focus on what's happening in the world, you'll find plenty to be insecure and anxious about. The earth is in upheaval."

He adds, "Friend, we can't change the world, but we can trust the Father to guide us and help us make the right decisions in our relationships, our finances, and our vocations. So, no matter what happens today, trust Him. He alone sees the future and will keep you secure as you walk in the center of His will."

Therefore, be concerned with what is happening in your immediate world, your inner circle and become the master of maximizing every opportunity to achieve your life goals. Grasp every opportunity you can to make your world a happy and uncomplicated place. This practice will provide as many perfect moments as it's possible for a human being to have. Create your own "amor fati," your fate.

Maybe some areas of your life do not facilitate the inner peace you crave or the environmental peace and contentment you must have to live your life to the fullest. As you consider making changes, take just a little time to formulate effective and practical goals. I would love it if you started keeping a Change Journal. This can be a small notebook, sticky notes on your computer or refrigerator, or you can also choose to use your phone and a journal like I do. I prefer a pretty journal that I can touch and admire—but select whatever will work for YOU. It doesn't have to be anything fancy; however, ensure it is something pretty. It helps when we surround ourselves with a few simple items that bring us joy and remind us to be grateful.

For me, it's books that are beautiful inside and outside; some books are for the bedroom, and others are for the family library. My list also includes candles, baskets, bookmarks, flowers, and other things that make me feel good. So, choose items that bring joy. Hopefully, your books will include a Bible and, of course, this book you are reading!

I always try to find pleasure in these simple and inexpensive "things." Maybe you already have a journal somewhere someone gave you, which you thought you would never use. Bring it out, make one with a few pages from your printer, or take a simple notebook and put your favorite pictures or prints—let's enjoy this journey. Make an intentional decision to become emotionally and spiritually stronger to live your best life and cope well with whatever life throws at you each day! Perception is powerful, so focus on every positive aspect of your daily life and create your unique worldview! This is a great coping strategy.

Formulate Goals You Can TRUST

This section is very important because it will guide your change process. I want you to formulate goals you can trust to guide you on this path you have decided to take. When you take the time to think about how you would genuinely like your life to be, setting goals that you trust will reflect your values and the roadmap for your life. Setting goals, you TRUST will bring out the best of you!

> *"Without TRUST, the best we can do is compromise; without TRUST, we lack the credibility for open mutual learning and communication and real creativity."*
>
> — *Stephen Covey.*

Your goals don't have to be fancy; write them simply and honestly as you reflect on what you want to accomplish. Let this table below guide you. It is my very own recipe for successful goal-setting that I have created just for you!

Set goals you can TRUST to take you exactly where you want to go on your personal or professional journey:

T Target the change you desire

R Relish each small step that takes you there

U Understand that you have the power to grow and change

S Seek to fulfill each goal you have identified.

T Take action!

This transformation will shape your life—make a commitment to start your journey.

Dare to Become a Master of Goal-Setting

You must fully understand the change you wish to make to set a meaningful goal. So, don't just think, "I want to spend more time with the kids," or "I want to improve my communication skills," or our favorite, "I want to lose weight." These thoughts are far too general.

You should think in more specific terms and target the exact change you wish to make. So, instead of saying or writing (which I strongly recommend that you do), "I want to spend more time with the kids," say or write, "I am going to set aside one hour (state the time you can realistically spend with them) each day to spend time with the kids." You can also add a helpful note about exactly how you will utilize the hour. Maybe you will go to a park, play a board game, build a puzzle, watch a movie, have a conversation, go out to eat, or do something else. However you choose to spend this time, remember those exact moments will never come back but will be lasting memories for your children and you, as you look back at life with them later.

If the desired change will be effective, you need to set yourself up for success. Be realistic. Think of how much time you can spend with them. Then analyze what you want to spend the time doing. Are you going to read to them at bedtime? Are you going to play a video game? Are you going to have an age-appropriate discussion about friends or school? Consider the ages of your children, their needs, and your schedule.

I suggest thinking about their needs as you decide because if they are little couch potatoes in the making, you probably think they spend too much time watching TV or playing video games. You can take them walking, go to a nearby park, or set up a basketball hoop or some other activity in your yard if you are blessed with one. There are also small basketball hoops for inside your house or apartment. They need your full attention for that time you set aside. Children need our time as much as they need food. Put this goal on your calendar as you do with essential meetings and events.

You can even choose to build a puzzle or play ping pong. Pick simple activities, keep them simple, and focus on the quality of the time you are giving. If you find it challenging to set aside the time exclusively, then you can spend time together preparing a snack or a meal, at least sometimes; get them involved. Let them set the table—being together and teaching life skills is what's important. Also, consider the interests of your children. If they like to read, a trip to the local library once a week may be a good idea. So, consider the ages of the children, the amount of time you have, and how you wish to spend the time together. Then, set your goal. If you do this wisely, spending time with your family members can be fun instead of frustrating, and this is growth for you.

Change Small Habits and Get Big Results with Short-Term Goals

I am always so grateful for the habit of making my bed each morning. It's a small thing that can give you a great start because it involves self-discipline. Another habit I wanted to change was drinking more tea and less coffee. For the past six years, an inner voice has told me to stop drinking coffee. I love coffee, but it appears that coffee has stopped liking me.

I guess my nervous disposition and my family condition, High Blood Pressure, may explain why. My second husband was from Wolverhampton, England, and I was an avid tea drinker. Years later, after his death, I lived with my second daughter, her Puerto Rican/Cuban American husband, and their seven children in a large older house in Florida I had managed to buy as a foreclosure after I sold my daycare center in T&T. They needed my help and support. I needed their company and emotional support.

It was a perfect interdependent and synergistic relationship that worked for us for a few years. Each morning, I would wake up to the smell of wonderful coffee, and I converted. Ten years later, I am discovering firsthand how tough a little change can be! I am getting there, but this is one instance when incremental change is not working for me. Sometimes, we need to make that 100-degree change without compromise. Wish me luck! I still love my one cup of coffee every morning.

I Learned to Cook Despite My Fear

I love breakfast, and although cooking has never excited me as much as it did my first daughter and third husband, I wanted to conquer my fear of cooking. I love breakfast and brunch and felt comfortable preparing these. But fear kept me from cooking for many years. It didn't help when family members teased me when I threatened to cook. I finally got the chance to live alone and recently discovered how fantastic it is to overcome the fear of failure. I relished making my first banana bread. Then I tried a T&T stewed chicken, and a T&T curried chicken. I am not upset that I didn't try before, but I am amazed at how fear and a lack of confidence can hinder us from trying new things. I hope you will overcome any fears you harbor and feel the thrill when you finally can overcome these fears. Now is a good time to reflect on the changes that fear is preventing.

Learn To Say 'No' With Grace

Throughout my life, I almost always said yes to my children's and grandchildren's wishes, although on many occasions, this meant inconvenience and even hardship at times. I would agree to family trips or looking after grandkids even when I did not want to participate or was not physically up to it. Now, I can choose not to participate without feeling guilty. I have also learned to say no to others, but always being gracious is a good idea. "I would love to, but I can't this time" is a good way to refuse an invitation without hurting someone's feelings. Over time, people get used to knowing that you will be honest about your feelings, and they respect you for your honesty and for thinking of your well-being.

Set Other Successful Goals

Now, if you want to improve your communication skills, take some time to figure out precisely what areas of communication you want to improve. Do you want to be a better listener? Do you want to improve your public speaking skills? Or do you want to make more time to communicate more effectively with others instead of sending e-mail? When you determine the specific area of change, set your goal. Remember, it will take some time to change your behavior. Rome was not built in a day, so aim for incremental change.

If you want to improve your listening skills, begin to practice:

- Focus on what the other person is saying to you and practice, practice, practice listening attentively.

- Listen from your heart. Listen with your heart, and that person or that child will feel at that moment that he or she is the only one who matters to you. That's a good feeling to generate in those we love—and even those we want to love.

- Become an empathetic listener.

How to Become an Empathetic Listener

If you genuinely want to improve, the first step is to think about this aspect of your communication and determine whether you are completely satisfied or can be a better listener. Once you determine that there is room for growth, the following seven tips will prove to be very helpful.

1. Make appropriate eye contact with the person. Listening with grace and caring always creates a win-win situation.

2. Show genuine interest. The other person will sense your disinterest or your genuine desire to communicate.

3. Remember the power you hold to influence someone positively or negatively by listening closely and with genuine interest and empathy if necessary.

4. Make every effort not to be an interrupter. I am still working on this because I am always so eager to share my thoughts and opinions, but this can seriously hamper our ability to really understand what the other person is trying to convey.

5. Strive to be non-judgmental; this will make you unique and highly appreciated because often, we are constantly evaluated and judged. Be the exception.

6. Make the other person feel that he or she is the only person in the world at that moment when you are giving him or her time and attention, and you have become an effective listener!

7. Continue to improve with each interpersonal interaction and practice, practice, practice.

Having someone give you their undivided attention by listening to what you have to say can be magical.

Think about how many opportunities we miss daily to make the people in our lives feel worthy, respected, valued, and loved because we do not listen as well as we can or should. Of course, this is not deliberate. In some cases, we have forgotten; in other cases, we are isolated at work, and then we have so much to say when we do have a chance to talk, we forget how to listen.

In today's busy, high-tech, complex, and often troubled world, having someone listen to us and "attend" to what we are saying has become rare. So, any time we give someone our full, undivided attention, that person feels appreciated and valued. Listening becomes a magical potion that can stimulate, motivate, and sustain us as we face daily challenges. The good news is that we can always listen actively to others if we practice. We really can go around helping to make people at home and work feel better about their days and their lives.

If you want to improve your public speaking skills, check out your local university and enroll in a public speaking class. You can also check online to see what is available in your area, and your local newspapers can be beneficial. Suppose you want to communicate more with your loved ones or colleagues. In that case, you can set simple goals like writing, calling, or visiting a particular person, depending on the situation. You may also want to examine how you communicate. Do you make eye contact? Do you close the door and give the other person your undivided attention? Clarify first and then formulate your goal.

Give Yourself the Gift of Flexibility

Again, one necessary ingredient for this recipe to work well is flexibility. I advocate goal-setting, but at the same time, I don't want us to become so overtaken with achievement that we forget to have fun. Too often, as has happened to me, we are so consumed with kids, work, and problems that there is no fun in our lives.

I like to think of a circle with sections or slices representing my life's various areas. See below for how my daughter, a working professional with seven children, used to see her busy and demanding life before she became intentional about making some strategic and positive changes.

Then please complete the same process that represents how you currently share the slices of your life between your partner, children, grandchildren, elderly parents, work, friends, and colleagues—is there a slice of life for you? How small or large is that slice? How does your life circle look?

Lisa's Life Circle

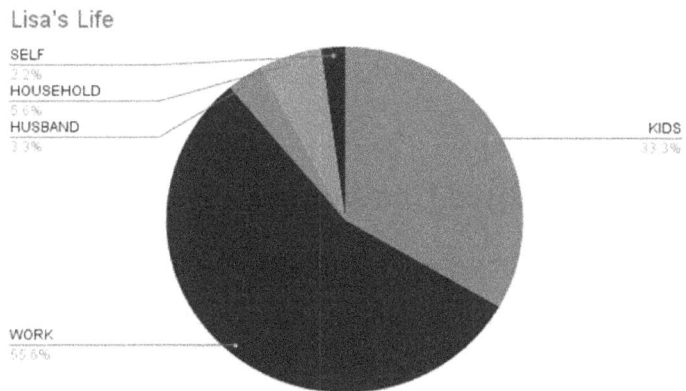

I use this to check the amount of life balance I have. If one portion of our circle is out of sync, you can make changes to adapt. No goal is written in stone—make small changes and adapt as you go along. One of our greatest strengths is the ability to adapt to people and situations!

So, adapt and be flexible, and when you check your circle of life balance, please ensure that there is a little portion in there for fun, or you could begin to feel like an empty shell with nothing to give to anyone else. Remember that you can give to others only when your cup is filled with friends, fun, and what makes you smile.

Set reasonable goals but revisit those goals as often as you like. Review and revise your plan of action as frequently as you wish. Make your own rules as long as you take action.

Just be honest with one person, always—yourself. Be flexible and set goals that will enhance your life and the lives of those around you. Always strive to surround yourself with supportive people who will enhance your life. If a person brings misery, you may want to set a goal to keep some distance between you and the person so that you can achieve those life goals that bring you joy. Identify the actions, activities, and people who bring joy into your life and allow and encourage these to impose.

Understand 'Delayed Gratification'

The concept of "delayed gratification" is fundamental to good goal-setting. Realize that we will not always get what we want when we want it. We cultivate increased strength and character when we learn to embrace the virtue of patience. These old sayings always make so much sense to me, and yes, I have found that patience is a virtue—and one that is wonderful to acquire. Practice makes one patient! And, very often, good things come to those who wait.

I have always wanted to write and get my books published, but raising children, work, divorce, financial woes, returning to school as an adult student, and many other life challenges prevented me from fulfilling this goal. I was always writing an article here and there, but the business of publishing the books I had been writing had to be delayed. There were occasions when I thought of giving up, but I kept on writing, hoping, and praying that I would have the opportunity to dedicate the necessary time and effort to the publication of my work. I was determined to share the life lessons I learned throughout my challenging, exciting, and adventurous years. I learned the true meaning of delayed gratification and never gave up. You can, too!

FROM SELF-CARE TO SELF-MASTERY

We don't like to wait, but sometimes we don't have a choice. Our technological world has not made this truth any easier. The pace of everything today rewards instant gratification, and when this is not satisfied, anger and dissatisfaction step in to steal our joy. When stumbling blocks arise, we respond with impatience, and if we do not accept that everything is not always readily available or possible, a type of misery occurs. These unhappy feelings of hopelessness, disappointment, and helplessness can be avoided if we practice self-discipline and mutual respect and consciously learn to adapt to difficult situations.

Patience and persistence are the keys to getting where you wish to go as you pursue your goals confidently and clearly.

In addition to everything I have shared, remember to never give up on a goal you have taken the time to set, if it's one that's dear to your heart. You might not succeed immediately, but you should never give up if the goal is essential to living a better life. In a Lifetime movie, a mother who died left a message for her son, who wanted to give up on his goal to become a great swimmer. She had written to him, "Our greatest strength lies not in never falling, but in rising every time we fall." I wrote that down and use it to this day when I don't successfully fulfill a goal immediately. I hope you will remember this quote as you move forward.

"Our greatest glory is not in never falling, but in rising every time we fall..."

— *Confucius*

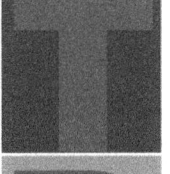
Target the real change you desire

Relish each step that takes you there

Understand that you have the power to grow & change

Seek to fulfill and satisfy each goal you identiofied

Make a commitment - this will change your life!

Chapter Three

Create Your Sanctuary of Peace

As I write, I am sitting at my kitchen counter with the sound of the whirring dishwasher in the background. That and the purr of the AC unit are the only sounds. I am overjoyed about being alone. I am mentally and emotionally at peace, at least for now. It's a perfect moment!

I interrupt my writing briefly to send a 'Happy Friday' greeting to my youngest daughter, who lives in another state. I started this ritual, and now she looks forward to these Friday emojis. If I don't send one, I may incur a curt reminder. One Friday, I forgot, and that day, she sent me a beautiful Happy Friday image instead of a curt message. That made me very happy. What an excellent way to jog my memory. Of course, I preferred that instead of any gentle admonishments.

With five children, nine grandchildren, and many relatives, finding alone time has been a challenge. If you are like me and relish being by yourself sometimes, try hard to make this happen. I have been forced to be creative throughout the years to carve out my peace because I don't believe we can become our best without this. I have learned, however, that we need to consciously and conscientiously create that tranquility even during chaos. The personal strength and quiet power that come from inner peace should not be underestimated.

Strive to become mentally and emotionally strong so that you can enjoy feeling calm even when you are in a crowded room or going through tough times. When you are gifted the quiet times like I am right now, be aware of them and definitely celebrate and enjoy them. These times are also great for quiet self-examination, as peace is essential for self-renewal.

I hope you find the perfect time to formulate your goals and set yourself up for success! If it's not an ideal time for you, there may be one small action you can take to make a start. Begin with any small step that works for you right now but do begin your journey of growth and change. We can always be better as we efficiently remove the roadblocks in our path, clarify our true purpose, and perhaps have a new vision for improving our daily joy.

Give Yourself the Right Beginning

The first step is to ensure that your home environment is a source of comfort, support, and motivation, one that provides a sanctuary from everything else, one that is safe, and one that will nurture your physical, emotional, social, psychological, and spiritual needs. Do you agree?

I stress "your" because I believe everyone else in and out of the home benefits when we, the adults, are happy and doing well. When your cup is full and overflowing, you can be present for family, friends, colleagues, and life partners. Being genuinely present in our homes is a precious gift to loved ones and others in our lives.

It is such a necessity in today's world for you (and those you love) to have a safe space, one where you can all look forward to going and being, one where you know that there is unconditional love and no one to judge, criticize or abuse you physically, verbally, or emotionally. How can you accomplish this?

Your Physical Environment: Decluttering is a Great Start

Like Abraham Maslow, I believe in fulfilling those basic needs first, so a functional physical environment is essential for you to grow and flourish. Let us not underestimate the importance of having organization in our lives. An effectively arranged desk, car, closet, room, and especially a well-organized home energizes and empowers us to live and thrive.

"If both the physiological and the safety needs are well gratified, then love and affection and belongingness needs will emerge, and the whole cycle already described will repeat itself with this new center. Now the person will feel keen,"

— Abraham Maslow

If your environment is cluttered, decluttering will certainly lift your mood—but don't try to achieve this in a day or two. Take the time to enjoy the process and remember there are always people who are happy to have the things we no longer need.

Whether you live in a room, apartment, tiny house, or mansion, you can have a clean, organized, and peaceful space. Whatever the size or location of your living accommodation, make it a space that you will love going to. Make it more – make it your sanctuary.

If you have a family, every member should help create and sustain this sanctuary; everyone should contribute. Don't wait until your kids are teenagers to assign responsibilities as this will be very tough—not impossible, but trickier than starting when they are young.

Everyone can help you do something, and I assure you they will thank you later. They will be grateful you taught them to appreciate and value a clean, organized, pleasant, and functional environment. It is wise for everyone to work towards this achievement. As a leader, you should always strive to be an example as your children constantly learn from you. You are shaping their future maps, a remarkable but scary responsibility. All will be well if you give it your best shot.

Children want to be involved, but they must be given the opportunity and encouraged. Growing up, I was very interested in cooking, and my mom, whom I love dearly, would always tell me, "I don't need any help. Go study." So, I studied and was very successful, but I still resent that I was married and had no cooking skills.

In fact, I lacked confidence for a long time. During my seven years as a flight attendant, I was always uncomfortable making and serving hot coffee or working first class, where the meal service demanded a little more than pushing a trolley with trays of food. I was thankful to know that my presence on the aircraft was primarily to ensure that the passengers were safe and that I felt ready for any emergency that might have occurred. Still, it would have been good to have had those home-making skills. It would have provided some much-needed confidence in that area.

Your Emotional Stability: Create and Sustain a Non-Threatening Home Climate

This will provide the physical and emotional stability that every human needs for survival and success. Abraham Maslow's Hierarchy of Needs theory supports this claim. He states that before achieving self-actualization, humans must possess a sense of physical and emotional safety derived from food, shelter, and love. A quote from Saul McLeod, Ph.D., explains in greater detail, "From the bottom of the hierarchy upwards, the needs are physiological (food and clothing), safety (job security), love and belonging needs (friendship), esteem, and self-actualization. Needs lower down in the hierarchy must be satisfied before individuals can attend to higher needs."

He further supports my position about the need for human growth and development: "Maslow's theory differs from more purely physiological representations of human motivation because motivation is seen as being not just concerned with tension reduction and survival but also with human growth and development." His article discusses "growth needs," and I encourage you to read it.

Achieving that positive and non-threatening environment essential for transformation to self-actualization may be less complicated if you live alone. If you have a family, it may take some work to create and sustain the level of peace and joy that you want and need to have in today's complex world. But it can be done. You can have a home that is a sanctuary despite the financial and emotional struggles that many families are experiencing today.

The following three practices will help:

- Practice mutual respect in the face of all hardships. When you talk or argue, do this in private. Children and family life are deeply affected by loud arguments. I have learned how emotionally damaging this can be to family life. Of course, if the children have stability most of the time, an occasional argument should not affect them, especially if normalcy resumes soon.

- Find time to communicate. Family members must find winning ways to talk and to listen to one another (more in chapter four). Do this while you can, as tomorrow is not promised. Learn to cherish each day and each family member.

- Don't be afraid to love one another (more in chapter seven) openly and consistently while you have the opportunity. The practice of love requires patience and kindness. Your life will be happier when you practice these and give them as daily gifts to your loved ones.

If you are fortunate to have a partner or help from other adult family members try to share responsibilities in the home, especially if you all work outside of the home. Do not run around trying to do everything yourself and then complain that no one is helping you. I have seen many examples of that. So, become a master delegator, strive for teamwork, and let all family members know that "Together, Everyone Achieves More."

I don't know who coined that phrase, but it is accurate, and you don't want to go around feeling like "Poor Me" when everyone gets comfortable with letting you do all the chores. I believe that you and your family should first discuss what chores need to be done, and decide officially who is responsible for what. There could be some negotiation as appropriate, but, in the end, just be fair, and everyone will be satisfied. Let family members know that you depend on them to do their part. Hold them accountable.

Here are a few tips about delegating:

Now, if you want to be a master delegator, you may have to take some time to communicate how you want to delegate an upcoming task. Don't expect everyone to know exactly how you want things done. How can they know if you have not taken the time to tell them? Be patient, and do not criticize when you delegate. Criticism is extremely damaging and will kill the motivation anyone has to help—words of encouragement, praise, and honest feedback when a job is done will make everyone in the home want to help you more! This will also contribute to a warm home environment.

10 Ways to Provide Honest Feedback Without Criticism

1. Start with the positive—find something positive to say, but remember that your body language also communicates, so mean what you say.
2. Try to provide feedback that is meaningful and constructive. Let the feedback be specific to the task at hand.
3. Be gracious. Even negative feedback does not hurt or embarrass us if we are told graciously.
4. Give honest feedback or trust will go out the window and be very hard to recapture.
5. Give feedback, positive or negative, promptly. Don't wait until you are angry, overwhelmed, or frustrated.
6. Eye contact is essential. Use it effectively.
7. Use age-appropriate words.
8. No comparisons, please!
9. Better to provide feedback privately, not at the dinner table—unless it's going to be positive and benefit everyone.
10. Make specific suggestions and recommendations to improve the child or partner's performance.

Of course, these skills that you teach family members while you establish your sanctuary at home will transfer to their homes and workplaces. They will become their skills for life, and everyone benefits! Unfortunately, negative practices like criticism are also learned and transferred.

The result can be dysfunctional families and workplaces so these patterns of behavior should be absolutely avoided.

Become a Master Delegator

According to Wikipedia, delegation means assigning any responsibility or authority to another person (usually from a manager to a subordinate) to carry out specific activities. It is one of the core concepts of management leadership. However, the person who delegated the work remains accountable for the outcome of the delegated work. The Dictionary meaning of the verb delegate is to "entrust a task or responsibility to another person, typically one who is less senior than oneself." Therefore, it makes sense to me that some form of "training" should take place, in this case, informally before tasks may be accomplished to meet our expectations.

Many of us delegate and then complain and/or criticize when the 'delegatee' does not get the job right.

Follow these 12 simple steps before delegating your tasks.

1. Invest some time in communicating what the task involves or spend some time training so that your expectations are clear.
2. Have realistic expectations until your child and other family members fully understand the task and your expectations.
3. Use age-appropriate language.

4. Be patient. You already know how to do the task; the person you are coaching does not.
5. Encourage, never criticize. Remember to say "thank you" for each small achievement.
6. Do not make comparisons. "Your brother would have already understood this" only hinders the other child's improvement and can prevent any kind of success at all.
7. Be compassionate, kind, and gracious, yet serious.
8. Be consistent and use simple, straightforward instructions while coaching or demonstrating. Keep it simple!
9. Refrain from shouting or losing your temper.
10. Always give honest feedback with a kind and gracious tone. Emphasize the child or partner's strengths!
11. Be willing to "let go" or "give up" some of your power and control of the delegated tasks.
12. Show your loved ones that you trust them with the tasks you have now delegated—when you are ready to trust.

You may wonder why I hope that you learn the art of delegation.

Learning to be an effective delegator will help make your home a sanctuary for you and your entire family as tasks will be shared. No one person will feel overwhelmed, burdened, or angry. Moreover, you are teaching your children, partner, and other family members to be self-sufficient—everyone wins.

We feel we are being mistreated when all the household chores are left to us. I certainly do. However, if we do not put something in place, the chores will be left to us, and it becomes more challenging to change when these patterns of unwillingness and/or laziness set in and take hold. Start soon—begin to delegate.

> *"Many people refuse to delegate to other people because they feel it takes too much time and effort and they could do the job better themselves. But effectively delegating to others is perhaps the single most powerful and high-leverage activity there is,"*
>
> — *Stephen Covey.*

Your Spiritual Sanctuary of Peace

Many adult children are returning to our homes. Many of you may be coping with taking care of kids and elderly parents simultaneously! Some are taking care of sick or disabled children and/or parents. My daughter works full-time as a Math Coach, lives almost an hour from her workplace, and has four active boys between 9 and 17 (plus three adult children who do not live with her). I see firsthand her struggles such as fulfilling household chores and other responsibilities like bill payments; she can hardly find time to converse or relax with a cup of coffee. As we saw in Lisa's Life Circle earlier in chapter two, she recently confessed that finding five minutes for herself is a real and serious challenge.

How does she cope? I asked.

She shared how important it was to be intentional, "To surround yourself with people who will be supportive and encouraging because this consistent support and the music and podcasts you listen to become very influential. These practices and choices affect you," she stated. She tries to remain uplifted by listening to spiritual and other comforting music; she avoids negativity and emphasizes how important it is to have family support. She states that she has deliberately chosen to surround herself with supportive and uplifting people as much as possible.

Growing my spirituality also helps me cope.

The peace I find from listening to spiritual songs and reading my favorite psalms (16, 143, 71) brings me spiritual, emotional, and mental peace. Of course, I also listen to other types of music, like oldies and jazz.

Regular Exercise is another coping mechanism for me. This provides mental, emotional, physical, and spiritual peace because it requires self-discipline.

Conscious efforts to practice kindness by giving time to others is another excellent way to grow spiritually. Finding the grace to forgive feeds our souls and allows us to live an abundant life.

A sanctuary is about creating an attitude and a conscious decision to find peace of mind wherever you happen to be. As my older son says, "It's not where you live but how you live." An excellent guide of encouragement for how we should strive to live is provided in the Bible. I frequently use this, the fruit of the Holy Spirit, to reflect on how I am conducting my everyday life: "love, joy, peace, patience, kindness, goodness, faithfulness, gentleness, self-control; against such there is no law." (Galatians 5:22-23)

Let your sanctuary be whatever works for you at this time and try always to be an excellent example to others. To survive and be well, you must have peace in your life; not having it will eventually affect your physical, emotional, and psychological health. So, create and maintain your sanctuary of peace starting today.

"There is no need to go to India or anywhere else to find peace. You will find that deep place of silence right in your room, your garden, or even your bathtub."

— *Elisabeth Kübler-Ross*

Remember to Practice Incremental Change

You will benefit significantly from having your own space. I smile when I recall that I could easily get my physical space in my first marriage when I had just one child. After that, I had to be very creative, and you can be, too, as you find ways to create your sanctuary of peace. That could be a spare room if you are fortunate to have that, a basement, or a space in an area of your house. I remember making a great home office and my sanctuary in my garage. That was **my** space; my five children were only allowed to visit for short periods when necessary. I loved having that space to myself.

Wherever you create your sanctuary, choose colors that will uplift you and keep things around that enlighten you emotionally and spiritually –perhaps your favorite books and magazines, baskets, candles, and flowers are all items that can give you a lift. You can purchase great keepsakes in garage sales, and this can be a fun activity for you and perhaps for the family.

We tend to think of our sanctuary as a place in our house, but it doesn't have to be. Sometimes, this may be impossible because of small children, marital problems, or other situations that make creating a sanctuary seem impossible.

Well then, primarily in these circumstances, you must find a safe place to find peace for at least some part of the day. This can be a favorite café, bookstore, church, or even a friend's house. When I had young children, I remember finding solace always in my best friend, who was single and unmarried at the time. Her place was so pretty and peaceful, and she always pampered me when I visited. I value those visits and the memories of those visits to this day. Thank you, Hazel Ward Redman.

It may take a lot more than de-cluttering your home to provide this sanctuary of peace that you so desire at this point in your life. Sometimes, being surrounded by the wrong person or persons can debilitate your sense of well-being and corrupt any chance you have of enlightenment. Creating this sanctuary of peace may force you to make tough choices about people in your life. But hold up and don't make any quick and easy decisions. Relationships, whether with your children, partner, or friends, take work, and let's ensure that you have been doing your part before you rush to judgment on who may be interfering with your peace.

It would help if you surrounded yourself with people who enhance your life. Be selective as you create your physical, emotional, and spiritual sanctuary. But make careful decisions about those who will share your sanctuary of peace.

Do note that you can pamper yourself when no one else can. Make that cup of tea—not just any tea, but the special one you bought. Have it in your favorite mug while you sit in your most comfortable chair and while you read one of your best-loved books, look at one of your most-liked shows, or call someone you know who would love to hear from you. Do the things that will nourish and sustain you as you strive to be your best and claim your "amor fati."

Do this one step at a time!

Chapter 4

Use Winning Ways to Talk and Listen

Having someone give you his or her undivided attention by listening to what you have to say can be magical. Think about how many opportunities we miss daily to make the people in our lives feel worthy, respected, valued, and loved because we do not listen as well as we can or should. Of course, this is not deliberate. In some cases, we have forgotten; in other cases, we are isolated at work, and when we do have a chance to talk, we have so much to say that we forget how to listen.

Right now, is an excellent time to think about the kind of listener you are.

- Do you listen while you look at the television or check your e-mail?

- Do people always preface their calls to you by saying, "I know you are busy, but…."

- Do your children often have to remind you that you did permit them to do this or that? (because you didn't really hear the request but responded anyway).

- Are you blatantly accused sometimes of not paying attention?

You may be missing great opportunities to respect and appreciate those around you. An essential part of living fully is listening carefully in order to respond appropriately. Don't be like the seventy-year-old who was crying out on her deathbed, "Help me! I don't want to die. I haven't lived."

So, are you up for a change? If you are, let's talk about some practical but effective ways to listen more actively.

Make Eye Contact that Counts

I know you've probably heard all this before, but making eye contact is essential in our everyday lives.

We don't like to admit this, but we all do so much better when we feel connected to others, have meaningful relationships, and make others feel good. One way to do this is appropriate and meaningful eye contact if this is culturally acceptable in your environment.

Remember to change the quality and length of the eye contact depending on what you want and need to communicate. This can be a powerful tool, so use it wisely. You know that, at times, a particular look can communicate so much: approval, disapproval, anger, pride, empathy, sadness, and more. We can speak with our eyes.

For example, if you are talking to your child, you may want to look at her with love. If you are a teacher and communicating with a student, this eye contact needs to be different, a mixture of caring and genuine interest. If you are in the process of disciplining the student, then your eyes will want to communicate serious business. With your spouse—depending on what the conversation is about, you also communicate with your eyes, and they do not lie. Our hearts can be seen through our eyes, so showing others how we feel and letting them know what we want to communicate can be done very effectively as we listen with our eyes.

We cannot fake sincerity.

Haven't you noticed that when we go to the bank or the supermarket, and someone takes the time to make eye contact or tell us to "have a nice day," it does make a difference, right? Even when it's nine at night, we can forgive them for telling us to have a nice day if they say it meaningfully and take the time to look at us –in the eye. Is it just me, or do we all feel better when we connect with others?

Whether doing an important job interview or shopping at our favorite store, we agree that an appropriate degree of eye contact is essential.

Become an Empathetic Listener

"If we can share our story with someone who responds with empathy and understanding, shame can't survive"….Daring Greatly: How the Courage to Be Vulnerable Transforms the Way We Live, Love, Parent, and Lead

— Brené Brown

Now, you have become even more aware of the importance of practicing appropriate eye contact.

Equally important is what I call sacred listening. I call it sacred because many of us do not listen to one another in today's busy world. We are either attending to the television, multitasking, texting, dialing a number, or occupied with something while we attempt to listen. This robs us of unique opportunities, especially with our children, partners, and colleagues.

We must all practice listening and "attending" to the person attempting to speak with us. I recently reread this in "The Road Less Traveled" (Scott Peck). I wish I had this wisdom in earlier years: "In a constructive marriage, the partners must regularly and, routinely, and predictably attend to each other and their relationship - no matter how they feel." In a relationship, people need to commit to listening and attending to the other person, and this takes courage, mutual respect, kindness, and patience—this is love.

We "attend" by giving the person speaking to us our undivided attention. We must either set aside what we are doing entirely for the moment or ask the person to return later when we can give them our attention. This is only fair and respectful, too.

In today's busy, high-tech, complex, and often troubled world, having someone listen to us and "attend" to what we are saying has become rare. So, any time we give someone our full, undivided attention, that person feels appreciated and valued. Listening becomes a magical potion that can stimulate, motivate, and sustain us as we face daily challenges. The good news is that we can keep doing this all the time if we practice, and we can go around helping people at home and at work feel better about their day and their lives.

Remember that practice will make this behavior perfect.

Listen Without Interrupting

Refrain from being an interrupter like I tend to be at times. I still have to work hard not to interrupt, and it takes an awareness of one's bad habits and a willingness to be humble enough to admit a fault.

Sometimes, I am so anxious to share I talk before the other person has finished their thought. This is annoying even to those who love me. I know that my efforts not to interrupt are appreciated. My youngest daughter would stop me with a hand gesture or tell me, "I am still talking," whenever I interrupted her. Her disapproval and my sincere desire to improve have helped me to make a change. I believe I interrupt less nowadays because I deliberately chose to change that bad habit.

How often have you been caught telling someone they look great when your face and eyes communicate something else? They can look at you and say, "No, I don't" because they have just seen the insincerity that your face and/or your eyes have shared with them. You ask your husband, "Honey, how do I look?" He responds,

"Great," but you change your outfit anyway. Something in his body language told you he did not mean that compliment wholeheartedly. We must realize that according to research, our bodies say more than our words at least sixty-seven percent of the time.

Sometimes it's hard, but do try a little honesty and sincerity.

Remember that we can say almost anything without being offensive or hurting the other person—if we say it "graciously." It works every time, and people will appreciate your honesty. They will come to you because you may be the one person who will tell them the truth with respect and in a manner that will not hurt or criticize.

Tech Talk and You: How to Choose an Appropriate Tone

In today's world of texting, emailing, and messaging, there may not be body language because they cannot see us (unless it's Skype or Facetime). But they can tell a lot through a little four-letter word called TONE.

Oh yes, just when you thought you could get away from telling the cold, hard truth, you may be surprised how much our recipients can learn because of the tone communicated through an electronic message or e-mail.

Always think of the recipient of your message, and choose an appropriate "voice." Your tone should depend on the nature of your relationship. If you are familiar with the person, then you can use a natural conversational tone, but if it's someone you hardly know, you will need to be more conservative and careful with the tone of your message. As long as you are respectful, your tone should be fine, and when you build a relationship with the recipient, your tone can be more relaxed.

It's all about building relationships, and when you take the time to do this, the benefits are great.

Be Assertive, Not Aggressive

When you understand the true difference, you will kick yourself for not practicing this skill all these years. If you have been doing so… good for you!

Assertive means talking or behaving with respect. Being aggressive means doing the same without respect, which is not a win-win situation. It can lead to misunderstandings, physical confrontations, and even disaster. Practicing assertive communication and behavior is the key to living well and peacefully.

A sincere apology can settle differences quickly and amicably.

I recall the day my car door barely touched the vehicle next to me. I heard the slight sound, but somehow, I knew that no damage had been done. Honestly, I did not check to see if the other car was damaged in any way. I would have known from the sound, but I should have checked anyway. Well, as I walked away, anxious to get into the pizza shop to place my order, a young woman confronted me in a very assertive manner, "You just hit my car."

I stopped in my tracks, shocked and slightly embarrassed because it must have appeared to her that I had hit her car and was irresponsibly walking away. I am still thankful that my response to her was, "Oh my goodness, I am so sorry. Let's see if there is any damage." Confident that there was no damage because the impact had not been loud, I wanted to appease her and avoid any loud argument. We examined her car, and she said, "OK, no damage. Cool, you are good." I smiled and was on my way to get pizza, promising myself that if my car ever touched another car, I would check for damage and see if the driver was sitting in her car so I could apologize. I was grateful that I was assertive and glad I was graceful in apologizing in this instance.

These small situations can quickly escalate into ugly scenarios.

Practice the Good, Old Ways

Write a note. Remember when you got that hand-written note from your boss, child, spouse, or co-worker? But then again, you probably never had the pleasure of getting a handwritten note. Take it from me. It feels great to get one and to write one. Call me old-fashioned, but I still keep a stack of thank you and all occasion cards in my desk drawer for when I want to show some special appreciation.

Remember, some of us will still appreciate a handwritten note or letter. Let's not lose these ways of communicating altogether. Save them for special occasions, but don't write them off. My neighbor still tells her friends about the handwritten get-well note she got from me after she broke her ankle while moving into her new house next to me! It meant so much to her.

Pick up the Phone

Now, you may prefer to text your Aunt Jennifer, who always keeps you on the phone for half an hour every time she calls. But there are ways you can get Aunt Jennifer off the phone. You can still have your cake and phone conversation, too, with just texting.

Suggestions for getting Aunt Jennifer off the phone:

"Auntie, it's good to hear from you, but I only have two minutes to talk. How are you doing?"

After listening for a few minutes, having given her the gift of enough time, say, "Auntie, it's so good to hear from you, but I must stop talking now." Of course, you may have to say this a few times, but make sure she hears you and, if necessary, say, "OK, Bye, I must go. Keep well."

"Auntie, apologies, but I am at work. I have to stop talking now." Hang up. Another tactic!

Remember to give your Auntie Jennifer the gift of time—that may be the last time. But in the interest of your time, be assertive.

Three Gentle Reminders

- Get off your chair and walk to the person's room or office.
- Don't always email if the person sits down the hall, even next door, or lives in the next room.
- Put the phones away at mealtimes. No one will die, and if they do, there's nothing you can do about it.

The Power of Silence

You are missing out if you have not yet discovered this powerful tool. Timing is essential if we want to be effective communicators. Do not underestimate the importance of this!

Whether it's your child, spouse, friend, employee, or colleague, holding back what you want to say at that moment could make or break its success. Think before you speak, especially if you are angry or too emotional. You may live to regret the repercussions if you don't practice self-discipline to say what you want or need to say just at the right time. Buy yourself some time.

A great practice is asking, "Can I think about that?" if you are unsure how to respond at that specific moment because your anger might cause you to respond irrationally. You will respond more appropriately later when you have had time to reflect.

This tactic could save a situation and avoid possible confrontation. Ask for time to think and allow your emotions to settle until you can talk and listen calmly and empathetically. You will be glad you did.

"Silence is not the absence of anything, but the presence of everything…"

— *Gordon Hempton*

Strive to be Nonjudgmental!

Being keenly aware of the areas you wish to grow and change is the right beginning on your journey to self-mastery. When you improve how you talk and listen, the quality of each relationship you have, personally and professionally, will improve; especially when you prove to be always non-judgmental from the heart.

This quality has been of special importance to me as I am deeply grateful to my children, grandchildren, many family members, friends, and colleagues who have not judged me for the poor choices and mistakes I have made at times in my personal life. I am always amazed and thankful that I'm respected, loved, appreciated, and valued because my personal life has not always adhered to social norms. I am thankful that loved ones have been nonjudgmental and have chosen to love me unconditionally. I suspect they realize that I have sincerely tried to learn from each mistake and strived to do better every step of the way. What more can anyone ask of us?

I do my utmost to pay this forward, and I encourage others to try not to be 'judgy' because, behind every face, there is almost always a story that we don't truly know or understand.

People can tell if you are sincere and not judging them. Then trust develops, allowing communication to flow freely. When this happens, everyone wins. So, listen with heart, and your genuine caring, concern, and empathy will shine through and overcome doubt and fear while building credibility and confidence. Effective, open, and honest communication wins every time.

Chapter 5

Maximize Your 24 Hours

If a loved one or one of my students or colleagues calls and prefaces the call with, "I know you are busy, but……." I always say, "I may be busy, but not too busy for you." On the other side, I can almost hear and feel the person relax. This makes me feel better because I am truly sad that many of us make the mistake of not managing our time efficiently to have more time for those crucial interactions with others.

I have observed a lot, and I see many who are continually busy but very unproductive when you look closely. Many employers have learned to look at a person's productivity and achievements instead of the number of hours they spend at work. They have realized the amount of time spent on phone calls, unwanted visits (because of an open office door), unproductive meetings, meaningless conversations, and other time wasters could be used more effectively.

The same can happen in our personal lives if we are unaware of our timewasters.

Think carefully about how you really want to spend your days. Are you allowing everyone and everything to manipulate your time? We need to be so mindful of each hour because it feels like you wake up on Monday, and then, without warning, it's Friday. We are left wondering where the week has gone. Be aware of your unique values and what things are important to you and yours. Then spend your time this way.

Save Time by Being Organized

We must be organized in today's highly competitive world. Living a well- ordered life is a monumental timesaver and one that is often overlooked. How can we be productive when our desks, cars, homes, and lives are in disarray, even chaotic? We will function but not to the best of our ability, and we will certainly not enjoy our lives as much because being disorganized decreases joy and productivity. A preacher once stated that "God is a God of Order," and that statement has stayed with me for many reasons because it just made sense.

I asked my older son, Richard, why he thought that statement resonated powerfully with me. He shared that living according to the ordinances proclaimed by our heavenly Father allows and encourages an organized, productive, and complete life.

Each person has her unique value system, and I respect that we have differences. Still, I have trouble understanding how one can function optimally without organization. I am not suggesting that we need to be compulsive about it, but we need to live our lives so that if another person needs to find something on our desk, in our car, or in our closet, they can do so.

I have done coaching and time management with attorneys who had piles and piles of paper, and they were the only ones who could find anything in their offices. The poor secretaries complained because this made their lives miserable and unproductive. When those attorneys were out of the office, finding a particular file took a great deal of time. Clients were not impressed by the waste of time, knowing full well that they were probably picking up the tab. Now, attorneys aren't the only guilty ones; we know that, but this example reminds us of how our behavior can impact those around us.

I have worked with families whose children will not and cannot bring their friends home because their homes are cluttered and in disarray, causing them to feel embarrassed. It's a serious situation when children cannot bring friends to their homes.

Take That First Step

So, where do you start if you want to manage your time and your life more effectively? My answer is, "One step at a time. Rome was not built in a day."

It took you some time to get here, and it will take you some time to make changes. The process is challenging, so there is often high resistance in people, families, and organizations. Change is also more demanding because adults must first unlearn old habits before learning or forming new habits. Nevertheless, this can happen once there is keen awareness and sincere desire.

In today's world, we must be efficient and effective. We should find the time to return each phone call, respond to important e-mail, and accomplish work and personal obligations; we need to take care of our homes, our children, our partners, our elderly parents; we must try to give back to our community and you should and must find time for one other person—yourself.

I am here to tell you that all this can be done—if you mean business.

Seven Ways to Take Control of Your Hours

1. Take time to develop a clear vision about your intimate journey. Utilize the results from your earlier and ongoing self-examination and reflection. Be proactive!

2. Understand what truly matters to you! Be specific about the changes you wish to make to feel more empowered about your life. Crave those changes!

3. Create and establish goals that you TRUST, which will enable you to achieve your vision, as this will keep you focused. Be deliberate and intentional!

4. Remember to prioritize based on your needs and desires. Make your unique plan of action!

5. Follow a few strict personal guidelines. Practice being open to growth and change and remember to note your accomplishments. Celebrate your wins!

6. Do your best to overcome any negative thoughts, self-doubt, and fears by having confidence in your wise choices. Own your decisions!

7. Live to your fullest potential. If, at first, you don't succeed, try, try again. "Rome wasn't built in a day." Stay positive and practice gratitude!

Far too many women and men have told me they cannot find the time to exercise.

Many have lamented that they have no energy for their partners once they climb into that bed. All they want to do is to be left alone. Couples don't go out because their days are filled, children feel angry, and many teenagers spend their time unproductively and recklessly. There isn't much time for family life or friends unless we consciously try.

We must find the time to do those things that are important to our families and us—before it is too late. The time for transformation is now! Tomorrow is not promised.

Seek Upliftment, even if For A Few Minutes

Regardless of how busy we are, let us remember to take a few minutes every day to marvel at the blueness and beauty of the sky, listen to the birds sing and watch the butterflies glide. Be in awe of the array of trees and the wonder of the seasons in whatever part of the universe you inhabit. Take time to relish the smells of freshly baked bread or newly cut grass. Take time to love the rain, the sun, and the moon, and listen to the sound of Barbara Streisand's voice as she proclaims, "Every time I hear a newborn baby cry or touch a leaf or see the sky, then I know why I believe."

Avoid Procrastination

If I do not enjoy or look forward to a task or if it makes me miserable to even think about doing it, I try to get that specific task off my list as soon as possible. That brings me relief, even joy. Try it. Instead of postponing the dreaded event, errand, or duty, try this tactic and see if it doesn't make you feel great when it becomes a habit. According to Brian Tracy, "Eat that frog!" You will feel so great and relieved when the most stressful task on your list is completed.

My Secret Strategies: How to Make the Most of Your 24-Hours

On those days when you have high energy, work twice as hard, and do twice as much, so on those lethargic days, you can choose to do only what must be done. Then, you can have time to do something to improve your day.

Please take the necessary time to get better organized. Initially, this may take a lot of time and hard work, but the rewards will be worth every second. Your self-esteem will heighten, and you will possess a new sense of well-being. You will feel more control over your life. You will feel great!

Create your tips and tricks to accomplish those big and small tasks. I will make a to-do list while waiting for someone or sitting in the doctor's office. During these 'down times,' I would also declutter my handbag, return phone calls, or respond to texts and emails.

Listen to the latest news so you keep aware of what's going on around you, or your favorite podcast or book while you drive. Of course, if you need to listen to your favorite playlist on a particular day, definitely do so.

Delegate all tasks that you cannot get done successfully to another person. Remember to show and express lots of appreciation so that others will always be glad to help. Tips and 'thank yous' go a long way!

If getting a particular task done will save time and anxiety, but you don't feel up to it, do it anyway. We both know that later, you will be glad you did. Self-discipline paves the way. Self-talk will get you off the bed or sofa and into the action that will make tomorrow better. You will smile when you wake up, and the sink is empty. You will feel great when the laundry is done, and Sunday rolls around. You are always glad you made that effort when you push yourself to shampoo your hair, even when you don't feel up to it. What's that old saying, "A stitch in time saves nine?"

We are fortunate to be living in these times, so utilize the services that can make your life easier. Now and then, order groceries or food online—you deserve a treat. If you can have that meeting or conversation online, this is just as effective and you will save yourself a forty-five-minute drive. If you are not up to going to a gym, watch a video and exercise at home sometimes like I do. Use the chat option to reach out to merchants and other service providers. I have discovered they are even more effective than those long phone calls with all the delays that make us crazy.

Now, you can spend the time you saved to have a bath, sip that extra cup of tea, watch a movie, take a nap, or do whatever brings you joy. You deserve it. Maximize every hour of every day!

The next time you have an appointment, plan to be early, not just on time. If you plan to be early, you will be on time.

Sometimes, we must say no, even to loved ones, when saying yes will intrude on other responsibilities and cause us to be inefficient or late.

The essence of effective time management and the key to maximizing your 24 hours is to strive to live an organized life. Be organized with everything you can control, and life will be easier to manage. Declutter, prioritize, set short-term and long-term goals. Use some planning tools if this will be helpful but always try to maintain some level of flexibility because you don't want to lose the joy that comes with building rich, meaningful relationships. You also do not want to miss any 'perfect moments.' The essence of great time management is self-mastery.

When you become the ultimate self-manager, managing your time will be a natural and very rewarding process.

"Lack of direction, not lack of time, is the problem. We all have twenty-four-hour days…"

— *Zig Ziglar*

Chapter 6

Increase Your Faith

I was an adult student in a graduate Psychology class at the University of Miami when a discussion about personal values emerged. Without hesitation, I stated that faith in God was at the top of my list. One student asked, "How do you express your faith?" Although I hadn't even started to consciously nurture my faith or spiritual development, I immediately and spontaneously answered, "By the way I treat people."

My response was from my heart, and this is why there was no hesitation in responding.

I cannot fully explain how my faith evolved. I am sure that having a single mother who endured so much hardship to raise her eight children helped. She believed in God and prayer, and her faith enabled her to overcome many life-changing difficulties, like the loss of the family home after my father died, and the poverty and challenges that followed.

I also spent five precious years at the best Catholic high school in T&T, St. Joseph's Convent. This school provided and facilitated an early education about the Bible, especially the Gospels of Matthew, Mark, Luke, John, and Acts of the Apostles. I was impressed and influenced by the stories of love and kindness demonstrated by Jesus Christ while He lived on earth.

My love for God continued to grow. Despite my inability to settle for imperfect and unfaithful husbands earlier in my life, I have always respected the second greatest commandment in the Bible, "Love thy neighbor as thyself."

I believe that love is the answer to so many human problems, and if I knew then what I know now, if I had the kind of wisdom that I have now about relationships and all that it takes to make them work, I would have made many wiser choices and had more realistic expectations.

It is heartening to learn about the great faith and efforts to grow spiritually from a few great leaders. Sir Martin Luther King, for example, is known for his dedication to prayer and spirituality and has been quoted as saying, "Faith is taking the first step even when you can't see the whole staircase."

You can tell that I like Dr Scott Peck. I value and share the philosophy expressed in his books about life and love. Like me, Peck believes there can be no profound or enduring self-development without spiritual development. In the preface of "The Road Less Traveled," he states, "As a psychiatrist, I feel it is important to mention at the outset two assumptions that underlie this book. One is that I make no distinction between the mind and the spirit and, therefore, no distinction between the process of achieving spiritual growth and achieving mental growth. They are one and the same."

Let me add that, especially in today's turbulent world, we need our heavenly Father's grace, wisdom, help, and continuous guidance. We need spiritual growth and mental stability. We need both.

Build a Relationship with God and Others

I always advise parents not to wait until there is a problem before visiting their child's teacher. Visit at the beginning of the school year, establish, and nurture an ongoing relationship built on mutual respect and meaningful communication. A neighbor should not wait until there is a hurricane to say hello, as happened to me after Hurricane Andrew in 1992 in Florida. Greet your neighbors and develop appropriate relationships. If you were there first, welcome them to the neighborhood, maybe take a gift, and let them know you are present.

A husband should not attend to his wife only when he is ready to have intercourse, and we should not call people only when we need a favor. Once, I called my mentor, Dr. Linda Howard, one of the kindest people I know, and she answered the phone by saying, "Hi Monica, what can I do for you?" I was surprised but managed to respond, "Absolutely nothing, Linda. I was just calling to say hello and thank you for the class you assigned to me." I could tell by the slight hesitation that she was used to students and faculty members calling her only when they needed something.

Sometimes, people do take advantage of kindness, but in the end, it still pays to be kind. I remember driving for over an hour to visit her when she was ill and hospitalized. I couldn't find the right hospital in Fort Lauderdale, Florida, and was lost for over an hour. Despite the frustration, I persisted and eventually got to visit and say goodbye.

I wanted her to know she was loved and valued by those who appreciated her kindness, those who did not look at kindness as weakness, and those who did not take kindness or kind acts for granted. I guess I simply wanted her to know how grateful I was that she "ignited the flame" within me by providing the prestigious opportunity to work with NSU's doctoral students for twenty years. This reminds me of what humanitarian Albert Schweitzer wrote, "Each of us has cause to think with deep gratitude of those who lighted the flame within us."

A few weeks later, at her burial, I was so happy that I had made that effort to see her when she was still alive. I always remind loved ones not to wait until someone's funeral to send flowers. Send them when the person is alive. Take the time to build relationships. Make time for kind words and acts! People need them. People remember them. It makes a positive difference in the lives of others.

Take a moment to greet the bank teller, the supermarket cashier, and the Uber driver. Say good day when you enter the doctor's office, even though you know that no one might answer. Do your part. Practice kindness. We all need it almost as much as we need food. We need food to grow, but we need kindness to thrive.

However, the most important and vital relationship we can have is with God.

We should not just go to Him or remember Him when we need something or are in trouble. We must nurture our relationship through prayer, meditation, music, and whatever works for us. But remain close to our heavenly Father so that when you call on Him, He knows exactly who you are.

Understand the Power of Faith

On so many occasions when difficulties confronted me, I had nothing and no one to count on but my faith in that higher power in whom I believed and trusted. Although there were many trials, problems were resolved, and challenging situations were conquered.

I may have fallen in weak moments, but I always found the strength to pick myself up, solve problems, and find ways to keep going. You have that inner strength, too. You simply need to believe in the strength of your God-given inner spirit.

Get in touch with that part of you that, as yet, may not be fully acknowledged and utilized. It's time to celebrate when we reach that point where nothing can really throw us down and render us helpless, even for a short period.

As you seek to nurture your faith, I guarantee there will be pain and suffering along your life's journey. But adversity only makes us stronger if we learn from each mistake or problem!

"Count it all joy, my brethren, when you meet various trials, for you know that the testing of your faith produces steadfastness. And let steadfastness have its full effect, that you may be perfect and complete, lacking in nothing"

— *James 1:24, RSV.*

How to grow and develop your inner spirit:

- Surround yourself with kind, like-minded people
- Seize every opportunity to educate yourself
- Learn to adapt to people and situations
- Terminate the "poor me" attitude
- Live with an attitude of continuous gratitude
- Become aware of your precious and perfect moments
- Make time to gaze at the wonder of the sky
- Be amazed by the smell of fresh-cut grass or the scent of freshly baked bread
- Count your blessings every day
- Live to your fullest potential
- Give thanks and praise to God
- Keep connected to God, family, neighbors, and friends
- Resolve to be kind in all that you do
- Practice forgiveness despite the challenge
- Spread love

These practices will help you become emotionally, mentally, and spiritually stronger. When we teach, we learn. When we love, we thrive. When we practice goodness and kindness, we are blessed with the profound growth of our inner spirit. Then, we can grow, make necessary positive changes, become our best selves, and achieve the self-mastery necessary to live fully despite whatever challenges emerge. Isn't this a great way to be?

"Your inner strength is your outer foundation."

— Allan Rufus

Clarify your Expectations About Life and Love

If you do this, it will save you a great deal of pain. Last year, two of my adult children stopped speaking to me for several months. Weren't it for my faith in God, I would not have survived this ordeal.

My children have always come first, and I could not understand this withdrawal of affection. Hopefully, you realize that I am always open to learning and growing. I have also learned to practice situational humility and consistent respect. When I confided my feelings of devastation to my youngest adult daughter, she recommended that now that my children were grown, I needed to "change my expectations" to safeguard my physical, mental, and emotional health. It was painful to admit that she was right.

During those months, I swear my survival depended solely on the kind of grace that only God can offer. You hear people saying, "By the grace of God," and my understanding of that phrase fully materialized. It was a very difficult experience, and I was thankful for my training in psychotherapy, which has helped me with self-management throughout the years. Making every effort to "practice what I preach" also helped with the reconciliation and forgiveness that every family needs to survive.

Thankfully, I have been able to grow and find joyful moments again. I have learned how to persevere by utilizing consistent prayer, exercise, and gratitude. You can do this too!

"Let your gratitude overflow into blessings, filling those around you…"

— Dr. Robert A. Emmons

Acknowledge the Power of Forgiveness

My two children were experiencing their life challenges, I learned, and unfortunately, some make the mistake of "punishing" their loved ones when they are suffering. They should understand that their actions inflict a great deal of pain and suffering. There were days when I did not want to leave my bed, but slowly, I began to look at this situation as an opportunity to grow!

I began to walk indoors with exercise videos when I did not have the strength to walk outside. On days when I did walk outside, the feeling of the wind on my face and the earth beneath my feet empowered me physically, emotionally, and mentally. I also listened to soothing music and consistently read my favorite Psalms and this book, "Everyday in His Presence" by Dr. Charles Stanley. I learned to appreciate nature more and found the variety of trees and plants spectacular. I yearned to walk on the beach and could do so only occasionally, but I was thankful for those times.

Unfortunately, Netflix became my best friend during those few months, and this was not good because it put my goal of publishing my books and writing on Medium, my newsletter, and my online courses on hold.

Thankfully, I realized that I needed to focus on a newfound goal that was essential to my personal and spiritual development. In the past, I recognized that I would always shut down emotionally whenever I was experiencing emotional turmoil. I wanted that to change. It is never too late to change, and I try to practice what I preach and model the way for family, friends, and clients. I wanted to change this. I wanted to be able to write and work even when I was in distress. This was my new short-term goal.

I resolved to work at it, humble myself, and accept that I did not necessarily come first in my adult children's lives. I had to give them the liberty to be themselves, make their mistakes, and make their decisions. Time is a great healer. Patience is a virtue. I practiced both, and healing has taken place, and our relationships are mending—but I have changed, I think, for the better.

I believe I am now guilt-free, and as my daughter suggested, I have altered my expectations by focusing almost fully on my goal of fulfilling my legacy—the writing and publishing of my work.

I could taste the growth and revel in my newfound excitement as I reshaped my life to live more fully during these golden years. I hope you will benefit from this shared experience if you need to reshape your life.

Increase Faith to Decrease FEAR and ANXIETY

With the scarcity of time and the transformation to an era of technology and globalization comes increased fear, stress, and anxiety about almost everything in today's competitive and complex environment. There is a great deal of fear, even among the very young, because as I write this book, two wars are taking place in Ukraine and Israel. The pain and suffering are palpable as we grapple with fear and uncertainty. Fear is in the air, and faith in God will be tested.

Additionally, so many younger people are dying from heart attacks, strokes, and drugs, and we constantly hear about mental, physical, and emotional diseases that we all must find the inner strength we possess to cope.

An informal survey from friends and clients suggests that some of the significant stressors we face today are financial, insufficient time to get everything done, challenges with interpersonal relationships at home and work, parenting issues, caring for kids and parents, coping with kids and technology use especially use/misuse of social media, uncertainty of the political climate, concern over racial injustice, severe changes in weather patterns, and the list goes on and is quite extensive. The current wars that are happening have added another dimension of fear and anxiety to what was already relatively high!

You will observe that we have more control over some of our stressors. This gives me hope, and I urge you to hold on tight to hope and not focus too much on those over which we have no control. Instead, become spiritually, emotionally, and physically stronger by taking superior care of the 'self' to cope with the unknown. Become an ultimate self-manager.

Pema Chodron shares, "Sticking with uncertainty, getting the knack of relaxing in the midst of chaos, learning not to panic - this is the spiritual path."

Walk off Your Stress and Anxiety

At thirty-two, I was an adult college student and single parent with four children, financial constraints, limited emotional support, and a household to manage. I had to learn to manage my stress and anxiety effectively or suffer the consequences of poor physical and mental health.

One day, I was so overwhelmed that I took to the street and just started to walk. I never stopped!

That was the beginning of a lifelong relationship with what has become a method of survival and my main form of exercise. I discovered the benefits of this simple, inexpensive form of exercise, one of the main ways to handle stress and anxiety. *I encourage you to "Eat, pray, and walk!"*

Nurture Your Faith With an Attitude of Gratitude

It is important to accept that stress is a part of our everyday lives. Of course, some days are going to be more stressful than others. I remember that not too long ago, I had three kids in college simultaneously, so I was working three jobs. It was a very stressful time, and it helped when I acknowledged and accepted it would be a tough time, but I always reminded myself that it would not be forever. This attitude helped me face the situation and make the best of it: being thankful that I got three jobs and had the good health and support I needed to work and travel as much as I did. This attitude of gratitude helped me face this tricky and challenging situation!

Remember that our attitude is the most crucial factor when we are overcome by tough times or confusing decisions. A grateful attitude will help us manage the stress of doing work we don't particularly enjoy and offer guidance before we make important decisions.

My youngest daughter gave me a little token of encouragement, Dr. Robert A. Emmons,' "The Little Book of Gratitude." and I share a memorable quote from him.

"Gratitude is not just good medicine, though a nice sentiment, a warm fuzzy feeling, or a strategy or tactic for being happier or healthier. It is also the truest approach to life. We did not create or fashion ourselves, and we did not get to where we are in life by ourselves. So, living in gratitude is living in truth. It is the most accurate and honest approach to life."

— Dr. Robert A. Emmons

Deal With Conflict Before It Explodes

When problems confront us, we can harbor some scary feelings. We wish we could just leave; sometimes, we put off dealing with situations and this causes them to deteriorate. After all, dealing with conflict is difficult, especially after a hard day's work. However, dealing with financial difficulties, relationship problems, and challenges with kids often worsens if we don't try to solve them as soon as possible.

Do your best to handle situations early before they get completely out of hand:

- Sometimes, it is wise if you are too angry or exhausted to buy a little time.

- Always let the other person know you need time to consider the situation.

- Communicate! When placed in a corner, always say, "Can I think about it and get back to you?" That position has saved me from making bad decisions and promises I could not keep.

- Confront each difficult Situation: Be a problem-solver.

When I say, "confront the situation," I simply mean that if we bravely face each stressful situation and accept that life—itself—will be filled with pain and joy, we will find effective ways to cope. Yes, life appears to be filled with problems; sometimes, they all come simultaneously. What can we do? How can we cope?

Strive to spend your time finding solutions and try not to complain too much, as this does not take us to any pleasant places. Our children will also watch our approach to problem-solving, so let us try to model the way. Momentarily, give in to the misery, but then call on the inner strength of spirit we all have and look at options and possible solutions!

Don't Limit Yourself

When you try to step forward into something new, there will almost always be naysayers, those hostile persons who will be discouraging. Heck, they may even call you crazy. Have the courage to make your own decision because, at the end of your venture, you will be the one who must live with your success or failure. Make the decision with which you are most comfortable after carefully examining all your options. Do a worst-case scenario. Ask yourself what you have to lose if you are not successful. If you can live with the consequences—in the event things don't work out as you hoped—go for it. Take the risk.

My attorney, with whom I would consult when making business decisions, looked at me one day and said, "Frankly, Monica, I don't know why you bother to ask me. You are going to do what you want anyway." My response was, "You are right, Raymond, because I have to live with the result of my decision, right?" He nodded in agreement and continued to provide his opinion, which I wanted.

Decision-making can be a long and stressful process, especially in challenging situations. Always give yourself the gift of time, when possible, consult with trusted individuals as necessary, and examine every option thoroughly. Then, revisit your decision as often as possible until you are comfortable. If you take these steps, you will be able to move forward with confidence and the knowledge that you made the best possible decision, and you will be able to accept the joy or the disappointment with the least possible stress.

Get Support from Your Community

I see individuals and people with a support system of family or church members, relatives, neighbors, and sound, reliable friends' function, and cope so much better than those who do not. Frankly, it's not possible to live and thrive without support. Take the time to put one in place before you have a dire need for it—because you will.

This is an excellent time to think about your support system. Do you have one? If not, contact friends, family members, colleagues, and neighbors and start creating one. *Do not wait for an emergency before you do this.* Make contact and keep in touch as needs arise because you may need to call someone. A list of dependable supporters will decrease stress, fear, and anxiety.

Take Timeout for You

You will learn about the certainty of burning out if you run around caring for everyone except yourself.

Burnout does not feel good. It makes you feel like an empty shell, and if you allow yourself to reach that point, you will have nothing to give to anyone. Medical problems can be very stressful. Have those regular preventive checkups recommended by medical professionals. I developed a habit of having an annual medical checkup a few days before my birthday. That has been my gift to myself for many years, and this practice makes me happy. I may never go on the day of my birthday, January 31st, but I always go at least in January.

I hope you adopt a good routine for your health and avoid the stress of illness as much as possible. Know when to take a day or even a few hours to replenish yourself when you cannot cope. Taking some timeout helps, and you gain the strength to start again. Please do not underestimate the power of timeout before you act under duress.

Develop an Action Plan to Cope with Ups and Downs

When we are in an undesirable situation, we must plan to get out of it one day. That might mean taking a course and returning to school—but do whatever it takes if you are miserable because the misery will only grow, and it's unfair to others or you. Moreover, the situation will be easier to bear once you have a plan.

A dependable roadmap will guide you, but please develop one that fits your abilities and unique destination. Let's use the same example of taking a course or returning to school. A great deal of thought is necessary, and I would recommend consultations with the person teaching the course or the personnel at the vocational school or college before enrollment. Don't make these significant, essential changes without some serious planning and actions. Consult as much as possible with people who show interest in what you wish to do. This will save a great deal of stress later.

Another example where an action plan helps is when parents must place their infant in a daycare center. I always recommend that parents invest their time checking out at least three centers before making that big decision. The same advice goes when you are about to purchase a house or apartment. Time invested is stressful, but it will save bigger stressors later if you develop an action plan and commit to it.

Handle Daily Stressors with Grace and Strength

I feel sad that we cannot escape the fear, anxiety, and threatening environment of today's stressful world. Rich and poor, old, and young – we all need to learn to increase our spiritual strength and improve coping skills to become stronger and deal with whatever challenges confront us on any given day.

The good news is that if we are genuinely open to growing and keeping strong physically, mentally, and spiritually, we can handle the daily stressors that will come. We must take advantage of God's spiritual strength, family unity, and a solid support system to help us cope.

Understanding the value of grace will also help. Dr. Scott Peck describes grace as "A powerful force originating outside of human consciousness which nurtures the spiritual growth of human beings." Like Peck, I believe our growth is stimulated by a force other than our conscious will.

In an article by John Baldoni, "The Attributes of Grace," he provided a very apt acronym for GRACE after describing this phenomenon:

- Grace is our path to comity, civility, and compassion.
- Grace is a catalyst for the "greater good" at work, at home, and in our communities.
- Grace is a clarion call for the goodness in the world around us as well as a practical guide to implementing grace in your own life.

GRACE is also an acronym representing five attributes:

G is for generosity, the will to do something more for others.

R is respect, the dignity of life and work.

A is action, the mechanism for change.

C is compassion, the concern for others.

E is energy, the spirit that catalyzes us.

I believe that we all experience God's grace at different times in our lives, but we need to remember to recognize and be aware of His blessings and kindness. If you believe in a higher power, I invite you to recall those moments in your life when you felt God's presence, power, and amazing grace. May we all continue to experience His love and grace.

"Faith is a living, daring confidence in God's grace, so sure and certain that a man could stake his life on it a thousand times."

— Martin Luther

Chapter 7

Become the Ultimate Self-Manager

I have discovered how essential it is to care for our bodies and minds by being forced to find creative ways to confront and deal with many life struggles. I was fortunate to have a great deal of professional support. However, the lack of emotional support from others who were overwhelmed from coping with their problems caused me to turn to God for support and forced me to develop my God-given inner strength and self-confidence to survive and flourish.

I feel compelled to -

- encourage you to attain self-mastery through the various practices and rituals I discovered.

- urge you to develop and practice self-discipline in almost all aspects of your life.

- encourage you to examine and understand your value system and your destination.

I ask you to consider the necessity to commit to growth and change. I greatly admire the authors, Dr. Stephen Covey, and Dr. Scott Peck, because of their faith in God and their noble contributions to human growth and development. I was gratified when Covey referred to the autobiography of Anwar Sadat, a past president of Egypt and stated that while he was in prison, he realized that "Real success is success with self. It's not in having things, but in having mastery, having victory over self."

Peck also supports my emphasis on the importance of self-discipline in our quest for self-mastery. He made the following statements that impressed me:

- The unceasing practice of discipline leads to mastery.
- Spiritually evolved people, by virtue of their discipline, mastery, and love, are people of extraordinary competence, and in their competence, they are called on to serve the world, and in their love, they answer the call.
- We cannot be a source of strength unless we nurture our strength.
- When we love ourselves, we attend to our own growth.

Another source that upholds my ardent belief in self-mastery occurred during my many years working with doctoral students at NSU. Most were leaders in corporations and the school system and were on a journey to learn, grow, and excel. For one of their assignments, they were given fifteen competencies that effective leaders should have. They were asked to choose the competency they thought was the most important. I expected them to choose 'technology skills,' and I was surprised and pleased when ninety percent of them selected self-mastery!

Finally, my motivation and deep belief in the need for self-mastery comes from the daily struggles I witness with clients and others close to me. I believe we can all find solutions to problems that will inevitably confront us through the practice of discipline, humility, and commitment to attain self-mastery and increased spirituality.

I urge you to develop the following seven powerful practices that will enable you to extract abundant joy and decrease pain and suffering in this life you have been gifted. These practices will provide the grace you need to use the seven chapters of this book to become ultimate self-managers.

"I have come to understand that the self, myself, is inherently sacred. By virtue of its own improbability, its own miracle, its own emergence. And so, I lift up my head, and I bear my own witness, with affection and tenderness and respect and compassion. And in so doing, I sanctify myself with my own grace,"

— *Ursula Goodenough*

The Final Seven Habits: The Essence of Self-Mastery

During my seven years as a flight attendant, I found flight emergency procedures demonstrated a perfect example of the importance and necessity of self-mastery. The emphasis there was always on putting on your own mask before helping anyone else—

you can't do much if you can't breathe. This observation taught me that we need to become the best versions of ourselves before we can initiate change in others.

In this book I am sharing the seven steps you need to follow to achieve self-mastery and in this final chapter I share seven habits I developed in my quest for self-mastery. I urge you to consider them for your intimate journey:

1. Exercise, eat well, and get organized
2. Get support during the change process
3. Become a lifelong learner
4. Connect with others
5. Pick yourself up when you fall
6. Make the decision to have a good attitude
7. Love your neighbor as yourself

1. Exercise, eat well, and get organized

Choose exercise that works for your lifestyle! I didn't always exercise. When I was in my thirties with five small children and faced with all kinds of stressors, including financial difficulties, relationship problems, and the challenge of living in a strange country, I discovered the need for exercise and the relief and positive results it can bring.

I was so burnt out that one day, I decided to leave the house and just "walk it off." I felt I just had to get some relief from all my anxiety. That was a keen discovery and the beginning of my walking journey—I have been walking ever since, and a regular brisk walk has become my premiere method of trying to keep fit and healthy.

I love to walk because it costs me nothing, but I must remind you to walk when and where it is safe. Choose the times and places you like—I love the flexibility this form of exercise offers. I walk outdoors because I love to feel the fresh air on my face. I love to marvel at the blueness of the sky, and I am always in awe at the wonder of the spectacular array of trees. I love to walk in a park, around a lake, or at the seaside.

"We are moved to awe and wonder at the grandeur and richness of natural beauty; it fills us with joy and thanksgiving,"

— *Ursula Goodenough*

When walking outdoors is impossible, I am content to use a treadmill or exercise alongside a good workout video. Additionally, you can move at any pace and walk alone, with someone, or even in a group. You can wear what you want according to the weather conditions or your unique style. Again, flexibility!

Research tells us that walking is one of the best forms of exercise, and I agree that even if you walk for half an hour three or four times a week, this can decrease your stress and increase your lifespan.

In the article, Walking: Trim your waistline, improve your health, written by the Mayo Clinic Staff, it states that "Physical activity doesn't need to be complicated. Something as simple as a daily brisk walk can help you live a healthier life," and provides a useful list of the benefits of regular brisk walking:

- Maintain a healthy weight and lose body fat
- Prevent or manage various conditions, including heart disease, stroke, high blood pressure, cancer, and type 2 diabetes.
- Improve cardiovascular fitness
- Strengthen your bones and muscles
- Improve muscle endurance
- Increase energy levels
- Improve your mood, cognition, memory, and sleep
- Improve your balance and coordination
- Strengthen immune system
- Reduce stress and tension

Now, this is not to say that other forms of exercise are any less valuable. Many people contend that swimming is the best form of exercise because you use every part of your body. Others claim that going to a gym is the best. I have seen others do very well with cycling, running, mountain climbing, and other delightful activities. Finding what fits your lifestyle is crucial and will not make you dread the event and the time it takes.

Make a choice that will work for you! Just keep moving to avoid inactivity. This action will prevent disease and add many good years to your life.

Try to Develop Better Eating Habits

You must know yourself well to select eating habits that will sustain you. I was a skinny kid and a thin young woman until after I had my last child. Then, I became aware for the first time in my life that I had to watch what I ate if I were to remain at a healthy weight. Despite all the literature, radio, and television programs, and, of course, the hearsay, be keenly aware of your body and unique needs and make decisions accordingly. You know your body better than anyone!

I do not believe in long-term dieting, but I do believe in lifestyle changes and moderation. I do not give up on eating anything I desire but practice moderation and portion control. I believe in eating small meals several times a day, and I believe in eating significant portions of fruit and veggies and fewer carbs. This has worked well for me because I can enjoy eating, maintain a healthy weight, and good health. Of course, I fall behind sometimes, as you probably will, but the important thing is to get back on track as soon as possible.

Remember that the practice of moderation is vital. I felt very proud recently when my seventeen-year-old grandson revealed at the dinner table that he told one of his classmates about his grandma's favorite, saying, "Moderation is the key!" This indeed served to strengthen my belief in that habit.

Get Organized: A Common Struggle for All of Us

Living an organized life will make the difference between success and failure—it is that important. Because we are so busy, things become neglected: a crowded desk, a cluttered closet, an untidy car, and soon these all add up and contribute first to a disorganized home and then—a disorganized life. It is urgent to set a goal to become organized or more organized as soon as possible!

Start small and feel the change sweep over you! It's like the feeling you get when you make your bed every day—it only gets better.

You will walk with more confidence. You will work more efficiently and effectively. Your children and others in the home will be influenced to follow your good example and will want to follow your style. My overwhelmed daughter, the one with seven children, has shared how making her bed, despite how busy she might be, inspires and motivates her to get a head start on having a great day! Try it.

Seven Benefits of Being More Organized

1. Increased productivity
2. Reduced stress
3. Better use of your valuable time
4. Improved sleep and rest
5. Development of a sense of well-being
6. Greater self-confidence
7. Overall joy

2. Get Support During the Change Process

We need a great deal of support, whether small or large, during the change process. Unfortunately, we are sometimes surrounded by nay-sayers who defeat and discourage us as we try to move forward.

Select one or two supportive people: friends, family, children, or colleagues who care about you and respect you enough to know that you are serious about the change you want and need to make for your mental and emotional health, and your self-esteem.

You will be more confident and content with your life when you love how you feel and look. Your entire outlook on life can change! Now is the time to be excited about becoming the best you can be—the power is in your hands. However, you do need support and encouragement to succeed.

Remember to turn to your greatest source of strength as I and many others have done when we realize we need support from a higher power. On the View, on October 16, 2023, Kerry Washington, author of her book, "Thicker than Water," was asked about her struggle with an eating disorder and shared, "My eating disorder was the first thing that really got me on my knees, praying for help, it was the beginning in many ways of my spiritual journey because I was like, I cannot fix this by myself. I am going to need help. That was an important time in my life. I went into therapy for the first time. I started really looking to a source greater than just myself and realizing that self-reliance is not the goal, that we heal in community and we heal in truth. That, I think, in some ways, was the beginning of my journey of realizing how much I wanted and needed more truth in my life. I didn't want to keep this disorder from people. I was never going to heal if I did."

"Don't be shy about asking for help. It doesn't mean you're weak. It only means you're wise"

— *Unknown*

3. Become a Lifelong Learner

Although today's world is so complex and turbulent at times, I feel blessed to live in an era of so much technological advancement. Almost every day, I discover some new technique that boggles my mind. I am continually blown away by how many opportunities we have at our fingertips—if we are open to learning. I feel lucky that I love to learn. I hope you do too because we no longer need to sit in a formal classroom or take an expensive course unless it is necessary.

We just need an internet connection and valuable information, online courses, seminars, and more resources are readily available. You may be shocked to see how much you can learn for free, or maybe you already know! People who teach and share information online are very generous. Even if there is a fee, you almost always have the option to pay it in installments. So much learning is readily available!

There were times when I hit the floor in my grief, but through education and a sound support system, I have found fulfillment and true contentment, and you can, too. Education is enlightenment; today, we all must be self-directed, life-long learners.

That does not mean we must spend years in a formal educational setting, although that can always be a plus. One can learn a lot from reading, listening to the radio, and watching specific television programs. Additionally, many classes are being offered today in community colleges and campuses everywhere.

Don't let fear prevent you from taking the first step.

I returned to school at the ripe old age of thirty-two when colleges were just beginning to market their programs to adult learners. I was among some of the first adults who had to mingle with the many eighteen-year-olds who were usually in college during the eighties.

Of course, I was scared and most surprised when I found that I could retain what I was learning quite quickly and bring much knowledge, expertise, and life experience to each class I took. I would be remiss if I did not include a quote from a book that helped me understand so much about the essence of adult learning, "The Adult Learner" by Knowles, Holton, and Swanson:

> *"An essential aspect of maturing is developing the ability to take increasing responsibility for our own lives—to become increasingly self-directed"*
>
> *— Malcolm Knowles*

I remember too well—how terrified I was when I decided to return to school as an adult who was a single mother with four little children. I also remember that armed with faith in God and myself, I traveled to a new country and transitioned from life in Trinidad and Tobago to the United States.

Get excited about all the fantastic opportunities available. Take a course. Get involved. Go back to school. Age is not a barrier. Knock on doors. Take charge of your goals and dreams you may have had to keep buried for years, like I did. The doors of growth and learning are now open to everyone!

4. Connect with Others

Sometimes, we don't realize how important human interaction is until we don't have it for a while. I have been teaching courses online for many years. While I was able to maintain meaningful relationships with my adult students, I cannot express how much I craved those face-to-face interactions.

We communicate so much more with our eyes, body language, and the energy generated when we have meaningful interactions All this is hard to replace. You will understand if you have seen the movie, "Cast Away" with Tom Hanks. His character needed to create "Wilson" from a ball to retain his sanity—he needed to connect!

How we connect is different for all of us, and this is fine, but we must connect if we are to live to our total capacity. If you disagree, I look forward to debating this topic with you.

We cannot always sit and wait to connect with others. We need to be proactive and seek out others in healthy and appropriate ways. These opportunities are right there, yet too many experience so much loneliness. Some say, "I have no money to go out all the time, so I stay home." This can be a cop-out because there may be someone who would love to come to your home and have a cup of tea, coffee, water, or whatever you have to offer. Try it.

You can also join an organization in your community. We discuss the growing crime situation in every sector, but we must play our part. Seek to become involved in a way that will make you happy and help your community. Volunteering, for example, is one promising avenue through which we can make this happen and give back to others to express gratitude for all we have been given.

If you like to garden, join a garden club; if you like to read, join a book club; if there isn't one in your community, start one. If you are older, there are organizations geared towards the elderly. Whether you join a women's club, start playing a sport, volunteer, or start a garden, there are many opportunities to connect and stay connected with others right now.

Are you feeling disconnected? Do you feel distant from your partner, children, colleagues, neighbors, family, and community? The time to take action and reconnect is right now, one person at a time.

Build a human network, starting with your family, then get involved.

Do not overlook the role of the churches in your neighborhood. It is a great place to start networking, as most churches have a group you can join. Whether you are a single mom, a teenager, or an older adult, there will be a place for you in the local church.

I encountered an office where two professionals worked on opposite sides of the hall and had never spoken. I have encountered people who lived next to one another for years without even saying hello. I lived in Florida for years—next to people who did not speak or say "Hi" to me until the devastation wreaked by the infamous hurricane Andrew in 1992. It was incredible for me to have neighbors come across and talk during and after the disaster. Looking back, I was just as responsible for the lack of interaction, but it seemed to be the norm on that street for people to keep to themselves.

I do realize now that I could have been an initiator. Don't wait like me; act now and learn from my mistakes.

The good news is that since then, many years later (it's never too late), I have made it my business to be proactive and have gone over and greeted neighbors who have turned out to be quite human and even friendly. It just feels good to do what is right; sometimes, we can't always wait for the other person to take the first step. So, be bold and take the first step when you can. You will find that people aren't always as serious or as distant as they may appear to be. Let's try not to always judge by what we see first, and let's not wait until there is a disaster to seek the company of others.

5. Pick Yourself Up When You Fall

Everywhere you go in today's world, you encounter stories of grief and personal challenges that seem too much to bear: children and adults with cancer, people dying needlessly from murder and suicide, young soldiers maimed for life, mere children being molested and raped, the proliferation of hunger and school violence, and the list can go on and on.

Closer to home, the cost of living keeps climbing as we struggle to keep our sanity, jobs, and marriages intact while caring for young children and elderly parents. We long for conversation and intimacy while loneliness lingers like an unwanted guest in our homes, sometimes even when people surround us.

We are so afraid to interrupt the lives of others because everyone is always too busy to talk, too busy to listen, and far too busy to share what has become a most precious commodity—their time. So, what do you do, in today's busy world, to maintain your sanity and cope in a world that keeps moving at a pace that constantly threatens to leave us behind?

The answer is to build and sustain your strength to feel empowered and able to cope in this changing world. You must be able to pick yourself up every time you falter, and you can.

Our lives just don't always go the way we want or plan. Because I always put my children first, even when they were grown, it seems that every time I devised a plan for myself, the goal was always so hard to attain.

This was easy to rationalize when I was younger, maybe because the kids were young. As I grew older, however, I got angry, even a little resentful, when I felt personally unfulfilled. What I am saying to you is what I have said to myself many times. Sometimes, we must do the most unselfish thing and put ourselves first, not all the time, but sometimes. After all, our children want to see us happy, and unless we are reasonably happy and content, we may not have much to give. Again, I always contend that our cups must be full and flowing over before we can give that 'overflow' to others.

So, I have found great joy in giving, but let us be careful to fill our cups physically, emotionally, and spiritually!! Then we would have lots to give, and we wouldn't have to keep picking ourselves up as often as I had to.

How often have I had to turn to God and ask for the strength to go on? The times are countless, but it is human to be weak; it is human to falter, and we must continually remind ourselves that life consists of 'ups and downs.' It is self-defeating when we expect our days to always be perfect. Let's expect perfect moments, maybe perfect days, but challenges will inevitably come, and we want to be spiritually, physically, and emotionally ready to pick ourselves up when we falter.

"Be grateful for the highs. Be grateful for the lows because it's in the lows when you learn," stated the late Suzanne Somers, movie star, business professional, and woman of courage who died in her sleep one day before her 77th birthday on October 15, 2023.

6. Make the Decision to Have a Good Attitude

From October 1998 to December 2003, I was extremely fortunate to work full-time with an international law firm. Then, I was truly blessed to start teaching doctoral-level students at Nova Southeastern University (NSU), and I also had a part-time private practice with another psychologist.

At one point, I remember packing my suitcase, going to the law firm on a Friday morning, and then leaving that afternoon for Las Vegas to facilitate a doctoral seminar for NSU. That meant being on my feet and being sharp for two full days, teaching daily, and grading papers by night. It also meant leaving on the red-eye flight on Monday morning to return to the law firm at 9.00 a.m. The real gem was that I also had three clients to see that evening for therapy. I did it and was happy to do it because I was thankful for my health and the strength to work. Again, a positive and humble attitude got me through one of the more stressful times of my life.

It also helps greatly if we choose to do the work we like. I know this is not always possible, and there will be times when we must work because we just need to earn a living—I have been there. But we do it to the best of our ability and again embrace the opportunity because we never know what that job we don't like can lead to. Remembering what William Arthur Ward said also helped, "Gratitude can transform common days into thanksgivings, turn routine jobs into joy, and change ordinary opportunities into blessings."

Try to understand and remember all the blessings we receive if we cultivate and practice being grateful. I encourage you to read *"The Little Book of Gratitude: Create a Life of Happiness and Wellbeing by Giving Thanks"* by Dr. Robert A. Emmons, and I provide some highlights here that helped me to develop my attitude of gratitude further:

- Gratitude is, first and foremost, a way of seeing that alters our gaze.

- The practice of gratitude is readily accessible and available to everyone. You are never too old, too young, too rich, or too poor to live gratefully.

- Gratitude enables a person to feel good and also to do good.

- Gratitude is the springboard for goodness and greatness.

- Without gratitude, it is impossible to flourish.

- Numerous psychological, physical, and social benefits are associated with gratitude.

- Gratitude empowers us to take charge of our emotional lives; consequently, our bodies reap the benefits.

- Gratitude increases self-esteem, enhances willpower, strengthens relationships, deepens spirituality, boosts creativity, and improves athletic and academic performance.

- Gratitude has fittingly been referred to as the quintessential positive trait, the amplifier of goodness in oneself, the world, and others, and as having the unique ability to heal, energize, and change lives.

- Gratitude is a daily discipline whereby you consciously and deliberately focus on all that is working in your life, the ordinary and the extraordinary.

- Gratitude drives a sense of purpose and a desire for change.

- People are more successful at reaching their goals when consciously practicing gratitude.

- Gratitude inspires good neighborly behavior—generosity, compassion, and charitable giving.

- When faced with adversity, gratitude helps us see the big picture and not feel overwhelmed by current setbacks.

- Gratitude can motivate us to tackle the challenges before us.

- There are two kinds of gratitude: the sudden kind we feel for what we receive and the larger kind we feel for what we give.

- Gratitude has been referred to as "the key that opens all the doors," that which "unlocks the fullness of life," and the "key to abundance, prosperity, and fulfillment."
- Gratitude powers our every interaction.
- Gratitude is the ultimate performance-enhancing substance.

"As the emotional force behind reciprocity, gratitude serves as a key link in the dynamic between receiving and giving."

— Dr. Robert A. Emmons

7. Love Your Neighbor as Yourself

What does it mean to love your neighbor as yourself? And who is your neighbor, anyway? Is it only someone who lives next door, or is it a "fellow citizen," as the US dictionary states? Have you heard of the story of "The Good Samaritan?"

The story is told in Luke 10:29–37: A man going from Jerusalem to Jericho is attacked by robbers who strip him and beat him. A priest and a Levite pass by without helping him. But a Samaritan stops and cares for him, taking him to an inn where the Samaritan pays for his care.

What is the central message of the Good Samaritan? Jesus used the Parable of the Good Samaritan as an example of loving those who may not be our friends. Jesus was asked to confirm what he meant by 'neighbor.' This was when He told the Parable of the Good Samaritan (Luke 10:25-37) to explain that people should love everyone, including their enemies. When Jesus Christ encouraged us to love our neighbor, He meant that we should have regard and respect for our fellow citizens and always strive to treat them how we want to be treated. And we all like to be treated well!

"So, whatever you wish that others would do to you, do also to them, for this is the Law and the Prophets." The Good News: This is literally "the golden rule" of the Bible. Do unto others as you would have them do unto you. In other words, if you want to be treated with kindness, be kind to others (Matthew 7:12).

Dr. Scott Peck also talks a great deal about the power of LOVE in his book, The Road Less Traveled………Saying that to love someone is easy, but love is more than feelings. Love is commitment.

Love is setting aside your own needs at times to minister to another person. Feelings can die, but if we commit to love our neighbor or whoever that other person is, love will not die. This is why some couples can continue to have amicable relationships even after separation or divorce. They can still love even when they have decided not to live in the same house or walk the same path. Their love must have been based on the practice of mutual respect and kindness, or they would not be able to continue to love after a decision to take separate paths. Divorce would not be as messy and painful if the commitment to love was honored. Violence would not be as prevalent.

Love also requires courage, doesn't it? Think about this. To commit to anything like a job, caring for children or parents, or even a commitment to exercise four times a week or dedicate time to prayer requires courage.

To love someone despite all their shortcomings and quirks requires even more courage. But think about the peace that love can bring!

Seven Requirements for LOVE

1. Love requires commitment
2. Love requires courage
3. Love requires abundant patience
4. Love requires mutual respect
5. Love requires listening
6. Love requires reciprocity
7. Love requires self-growth

"Love is patient and kind; love does not envy or boast; it is not arrogant or rude. It does not insist on its own way; it is not irritable or resentful; it does not rejoice at wrongdoing but rejoices with the truth."

— *(1 Corinthians 13:4–8a) (ESV)*

Go from Self-Care to Self-Mastery: Become the Ultimate Self-Manager

YOU HAVE ACHIEVED SELF MASTERY:

- when you become selfless and can make decisions on what's best for others
- when you can do good and allow others to enjoy the praise and recognition

- when you can forgive freely even if it takes time to do so in some instances
- when you can be humble
- when you can say 'I am sorry' from the heart
- when the practice of kindness brings you joy and peace
- when you truly believe in the practice of mutual respect and live accordingly
- when you realize that it is the color of a person's heart that really matters not the color of their skin
- when you can pick yourself up when you fall and keep walking tall in the face of adversity
- when you can love others the way God loves us

Everything I have shared so far can enable you to live the productive and full life that I wish for you—a life that you deserve and one that is filled with joy whether people surround you or not, whether you are solving a big problem or in the center of a stressful event in your personal and professional life. Covey supported this point by stating, "I am always amazed at the results that happen, both to individuals and to organizations, when responsible, proactive, self-directing individuals are turned loose on a task."

You fit this description perfectly when you become the ultimate self-manager!

You will live this full life because you have reflected and taken action to become your best self. Only when you have achieved self-mastery and control of your life can you truly give to others. When your cup is full and running over, you have much to give; only then can you practice respect—the beginning of real love and regard for your neighbor's well-being.

An outstanding attorney once asked me what quality I liked best about myself. I told him it was my ability to adapt to people and situations. This ability has enabled me to live and love fully and abundantly, creating my "amor fati."

Through many painful experiences, I discovered that true love cannot be based only on feelings but on careful decision-making, commitment, and hard but joyful work.

You can live fully, too! Transformation is magical.

From Self-Care to Self-Mastery

An Intimate Journey for Reflection and Action

We need more than self-care to survive and thrive in today's challenging world!

Monica invites you to reflect on the differences between self-care and self-mastery before you begin an intimate journey of honest and in-depth self-examination. These reflections will reveal the areas of your life you want to improve or change.

She provides a framework to help you set goals you can TRUST. She suggests ways to make your home a sanctuary of peace, winning ways to talk and listen with empathy, and strategies to maximize your twenty-four hours.

She hopes that through her stories and personal disclosures, you will increase your faith in God and aspire to be an ultimate self-manager.

Monica spent fifteen years as a high school teacher, flight attendant, and daycare center owner and director before immigrating to the United States to become a psychotherapist, adjunct professor, and professional development specialist.

She also worked as a radio and TV presenter in Trinidad and Tobago and is presently focused on developing her writing career, the next chapter of her leadership legacy, and the primary vehicle for the fulfillment of her current passion -- your achievement of self-mastery.

She is eager to share the benefits and lessons she has learned from her personal and professional journey and her experiences as a mother of five and grandmother of nine.

Live, Laugh, Love ! Become your best self.

Monica

From Self-Care to Self-Mastery

An Intimate Journey for Reflection and Action

For Monica's course and to sign up for her newsletter go to

www.selfmasterysanctuary.com

www.ingramcontent.com/pod-product-compliance
Lightning Source LLC
Chambersburg PA
CBHW071121090426
42736CB00012B/1976